RUSH of RIVER over ROCK

RUSH of RIVER over ROCK

SPINNING SEVENS
PRESS

ISBN 978-0-9845850-8-3

Designed by Chris Legg

Cover image by Carol Moates

Dedication

For my grandchildren
and
In loving memory of
my grandmothers
and of Luke

Publisher's Note

RUSH of RIVER over ROCK is a unique work—a fictionalized reality written by an equally unique woman who lived this story and loved the dog she called Luke. It is written in journal form by design, and as with many a personal journal, liberties are taken with the language which may raise the eyebrow of a grammatical purist. The text is fashioned so the voice of the narrator flows as the writer intended. The work is perhaps best considered a prose poem, a voice from the rural spaces of the Appalachian region, and it is left authentic to the author's intentions.

Acknowledgments

With much appreciation to Robert Wolff, for needed technical assistance and, even more, for the warmth of his encouragement, the sharing of broad experience of the world and his ability as both artist and writer. A particular thank you to him for suggesting the title of this story, taken from the manuscript.

To Natalie Smith for her many gifts, especially the unforgettably beautiful work of Cherokee contemporary art, Hives. And, with Leon Grodsky, the Lift Tribal Grounds Coffee House with its back porch on the Oconoluftee, a place to sit and write. Or just sit and watch the river.

Prologue

There is a ridge in the mountains of western North Carolina that is entrance to a farm. Deer leap and call on this ridge, Red Tail Hawk circle overhead and shrill their cry, bob cat make low, guttural mews in the night and sometimes startle with a scream, high pitched, alarming. After years of silence, elk hooves now strike the ground, quietly. Bear cross the ridge, unknown, other than their tracks.

Here, the moon hangs damp and close and stars seem near touching. An unseen life of night lingers in early dew, and the sun rises with ringing echo from two ridges and a river over where a farmer calls his cows. Unless fog has quieted the world, blue waves of successive mountains separate sky from all the tree tops that lie before it. The day's last color slips westward, behind a high place that humps large and green, protective.

Breeze skips up a pass to this ridge or shifts as wind that rushes from woods to the north. A narrow and unmaintained road, too steep in ice or mud for a Jeep, cuts to the house in a hollow below. There, as first color of August daybreak slants into opened and unshaded, second story windows, Ella awakens from a dream.

In the dream, Luke lay sleeping, wolf like, his head curled onto a large front paw, the outer coat of his double coat light in shining sunlight, the grass around him green as spring. He lifts his head and looks around with interest, up slanted eyes alert. He rises with strength and grace, pain and disability gone. He gets up easily and runs with full tail outstretched behind him. He runs like wind into distance of dream.

1993

March 14th

Snow began this morning and hasn't stopped. Flakes are large and wet, and by afternoon the hollow was alive with quietness, a silence almost audible, a presence like the dream I awakened from early this morning. In the fleeting dream, vague as mist, a wolf, large and light in color, stood among the dark, dark green of rhododendron hells on the north curving ridge that rises across from this house. The wolf was only a glimpse, a stationary figure, quickly gone. Yet the dream has stayed with me throughout the day, though wolves were killed out from these mountains long ago. As were the eagle, passenger pigeon, buffalo, cougar, elk, river otters, old growth forests, and many, many native people.

Well before dark, I brought in extra wood for the stoves and drew water in case electric lines go down and the pump no longer works. Then, I walked in thickening snow on the same north facing ridge of the dream and cut down to the curving river that almost rings the farm and its ridges that circle this small house. Shallow water washed gray over dark rocks, and the cold dampness went through me. Soon, I walked back up the old road bed towards home's warmth and raised my face to rapid snowflakes that stuck briefly to eyelashes and froze on the green wool beret covering the top of my head.

Here at the house, a pot of white bean soup, fragrant with bay leaves and fennel, waited on the warming shelf of the wood cook stove along with an iron skillet of crusty cornbread, a ceramic pot of butter on the kitchen table near by. The faint smell of lavender steamed from a kettle of water on the wood heat stove in the living room. With supper finished and dishes washed, I will soon soak in a warm bath and go up the cold stairway to bed where, even in weather like this, I like to sleep against the partly opened, double window of the unlighted and unheated room. I won't see stars or moon tonight and will put an extra wool comforter over the double wool futon on the iron bedstead. The warmth of this bed I slept in as a child, in my father's old cabin within sight of the river, is becoming familiar to me again.

March 15th

Here it is mid-March, before winter has iced us in. By us, I mean this place and the wildlife, since I'm the only person anywhere around. The snow began like earlier ones, wet flakes covering the Blue Ridge, the Smokies and valleys between mountains. But it didn't stop like other snows and, by this second afternoon, the accumulation is high on my thigh, deeper than I ever remember snow in these North Carolina mountains.

We've lost power, which this place is well set up for, with the smaller wood cook stove and larger wood heat stove. Tonight, I'll sleep on the futon sofa in the living room to keep the fire fed in the larger stove so that, hopefully, water pipes won't freeze. For the temperature has plummeted and wind turned icy. Since the electric pump to the spring is out, I'm bucketing water from it and am glad not to have a refrigerator to worry about. Wish I had gotten the higher spring gathered to come down to the house by gravity flow.

There's still a good store of grains and beans in the lard tins under the stairs, some potatoes, carrots and butter in the root cellar. Parsley in the cold frame is doing fine, and I picked a large bunch to put in water in the warmer living room where I'm writing tonight by solar flashlight. Here by the warm stove, in the comfortable old rocking chair bought for five dollars at a second hand store when Sarah was born, the rocker I nursed all four babies in. The children grew up and went out into the world, and the rocker has gone wherever I've lived. It must be at least a half century old now, like me.

March 16th

The hollow lies silent and clean. I tried to walk to the barn to check on the cats. Mostly, I wanted to see the extent of snow, for I know barn cats are good at taking care of themselves. The walk, up the winding dirt road that usually takes less than five minutes each way, turned into an hour and a half ordeal of trying to lift my legs out of deep snow. Drifts, blown by high winds, were the surprise. When I stumbled and fell into a drift covered gully, I had to fight my way out of dangerously deep snow. With nearest neighbors a mile away and the phone out, no one knew I was walking around on a ninety acre mountain farm with snow in unexpected places over my head. If I had broken a leg in the fall, I might not have gotten out. I haven't taken my usual walks up to the top of the high ridge each morning and evening, and won't attempt the barn again until snow melts. It has stopped coming down.

March 17th

My walks now are necessary ones over icy paths to get wood from the shed and water from the spring, both downhill from the house. The outlet pipe to the toilet froze and probably burst, so I make trips to the woods and have discovered that a bared bottom, though not very fat, doesn't get cold in icy wind. Much bathing is not even a consideration. Paths to the wood shed, spring and woods have become increasingly treacherous as the temperature fell to several degrees below zero last night and refroze surfaces somewhat softened during the day. I have no news of the storm, for I'd neglected radio batteries here at the end of winter. Though it is bitterly cold outside, I am staying warm and have plenty to eat. There was enough sunlight this afternoon to recharge solar lanterns somewhat, so I can read a short while in the evening.

I like the quietness.

March 18th

Today, I walked very carefully down the edge of the narrow and icy roadbed to the river. The water that usually rushes over rock was thickly frozen with barely discernible flow underneath midstream, something I've seen only once, many years ago. Several kinds of animal tracks were etched along the snow covered bank— huge inverted Vs of a buck deer and smaller ones of doe, three pointed raccoon tracks, a lovely abstract of bird feet. There was another small print that I didn't recognize and wonder if it were mink. I saw one in the river last summer and don't know if they hibernate in winter or not. The track is too small for an otter though I keep hoping that, someday, I will see one.

Each day now, I make new paths to the wood shed, spring and woods, as they refreeze to solid ice overnight. Fat, blue looking frozen cones, over two feet long, hang from the south facing roof of the house and outbuildings. Here in the house, it is an on going job to keep even the areas around the wood stoves warm, though the upstairs is shut off.

March 19th

Today, I used the last of the carrots and lemons. Still have a few onions left and plenty of grains and beans and salt. The rustles and pops of the fire in the wood stove beside me are company, and this rocker close to the stove is the only warm place in the house tonight. The outside Fahrenheit temperature is well below zero and the wind, fierce.

With the phone out and nothing at all coming down this old road bed that ends at the river, the aloneness is something I can almost touch. Sitting here by the stove, I write with my pad of paper on the rocker's wooden arm and just noticed that, with a small shift, the word "aloneness" becomes "all oneness." I've never noticed that before, yet do feel a oneness with this place, the land and wildlife though I've seen no animals since the snow fell. Other than birds that still come to the yard.

March 20th

On a back path that skirts the icy road bed and where a snow blanket is still thick, but softening and not heavily drifted, I walked to the barn again today. Carin's cats are fine. It was a purplish day, as though more snow might come, and didn't. Something about the late afternoon light turned snow lavender beneath orchid sky. A hawk flew over, not too high, and its tail looked violet rather than the usual reddish. As I walked back to the house, a short sun reached hollow's edge and even the shadowed tin roof of the house glowed purple.

March 21st

Deer and other tracks along the slowly thawing river are many, though I still haven't seen the deer I usually see. Nor have I attempted to walk the high ridge as I usually do, for it remains deep in snow or icy on its ascent. Telephone and radio are still out, so I have no news of the storm but do have enough basic food. I miss extras like butter and parsley, which froze in the cold frame. I used all the parsley I had picked, with no thought the cold and snow would last this long. What I really miss is a real bath and will work on that tomorrow.

March 22nd

It was an event, though jarring, when the phone rang about mid morning. Electricity remains out. Ruth called to check on me and, talking to her, I realized how regularly Elliot usually rides his tractor down the mile of unmaintained road between their house and this one. Often, his tractor will get down this old, shaded roadbed even when my Jeep won't go in or out. Casually, from the tractor's seat as I stand by the road, he will pass the time of day and then ask if I need fire wood, or a summer pasture mowed, help I appreciate. Not even Elliot's tractor has managed the icy roadbed this week.

Friends in town also called and said that Irish music, scheduled for the Pine Tavern Saturday night, is still on. Since today is only Thursday, I should be able to hike over the south facing ridge by Saturday and out to the gravel state road where the Jeep is parked. The state roads have been scraped, Ruth said, and with the small solar battery charger on the dashboard, the Jeep should start. I'll drive into town for supper and hear Will's good music and hike back from the state road onto the farm afterwards. I'm smiling at the thought of a moon lit walk on the ridge.

Also talked to Carin and found that everyone in the family is fine, snowed in but nothing like this. It still takes me by surprise that, with her birthday a few weeks ago, all four of my children are over twenty one and the older three, married.

Another big event for the day, which occupied a good part of the afternoon, was hauling in twelve gallons of water for a bath, in addition to the water I've been bucketing each day. And carrying in extra wood to heat the bath water, a lot of moving things about. But, oh, it will feel good in a few minutes to pour the last two heated bucketsful into the tub and soak by candlelight. And return tonight to the upstairs bedroom to sleep by a starry window.

My trodden paths are muddy now, rather than icy. Cold looking icicles hang from the south roof, yet are visibly smaller. At the river today, I could see more flow under the midstream, though it's still iced over. Shallow water pools along some of the bank. Deep snow remains on most of the farm, deeper in gullies, and the shaded, north facing road bed remains solid ice. It could be weeks, and with spring mud perhaps months, before I can get a plumber to drive down to fix the toilet. But I like a latrine open to the heavens, especially at bedtime when the sky is alive with stars.

Actually, it's not a latrine, for the ground has been too frozen to dig. For cover, I pry old leaves from icy ditches along the roadbed each day. I do still have some toilet paper and will go into town early enough Saturday to pick up groceries and supplies.

March 23rd

Electricity came back on today, but what mattered more was to see five deer on the high meadow when I walked up the ridge. Still snow covered, the pasture had patches of sun where grass shimmered and does grazed. As they got my scent, the deer raised their heads and returned to eating, instead of leaping off. I stopped and retraced steps a short way back down the ridge to stand and watch them. Two of the deer were smaller, almost yearlings. In several weeks, there should be new fawns hidden in tall grass or thickets.

These deer on the snow covered ridge brought back to me the memory of that first winter I spent here alone. Of the first night I hiked in over that high ridge, fairly late, after eating a birthday supper with friends at the Pine. Snow was deep that February night though no longer falling and not icy, nothing like this past week's storm. Yet the snow was deep enough that everything shone white, as far as I could see. A full moon intensified the startling whiteness, etched in memory like a black and white photo.

Halfway down the upper pasture, I had stopped that night and, with no forethought, called out to the deer. There weren't any deer in sight, but since summer I had mulled the problem that wildlife ate the garden and hadn't left enough food for me. To my own surprise, there on the bright moonlit pasture, I called aloud to the deer's unseen presence and asked their help to make this farm a sanctuary for all life, theirs lives and mine.

No Hunting signs have long been posted on the property, and I asked the deer that I couldn't see, but felt were there, to let other animals know they are protected here, too, and I need their help. I asked that they eat the ends of the garden rows and leave food for me. Since I don't eat the meadow grass and wild forage they do, I added as an after thought.

My voice, usually quiet, had risen on the wind and carried with it and when the sound of it stopped, I felt silly for calling out to others I couldn't even see. I still remember feeling foolish as I walked down the meadow and reached the turn in the path. From there, I glimpsed this house in the moonlit hollow below and felt the cold breath of the upper spring as I passed by, eager now to reach the warmth of home. Though I could see that the wood stove fire had gone out, for there was no smoke coming from the chimney. I still remember that.

Next morning before breakfast, as usual, I walked back up the ridge. As I rounded that damp curve of the spring and started up the steeper meadow, I saw above me eleven deer in a circle. They stood around the very place where I'd stood in the middle of the night before. I thought I must be seeing things, for never have I seen eleven deer together on any part of the farm, before or since, and none in a circle. I took a few steps, leaning forward, squinting my eyes in the sun to see if I really saw what I thought I did. The deer got my scent and bounded off into bordering woods.

The following summer nothing ate the garden, not even the ends of the rows. Not believing, I would go each morning to look and hold my breath approaching, afraid that broccoli would be sliced by sharp teeth and gone. Or that peas, fattening to full, had disappeared. Nothing ate the gardens that summer, or since, though it's probably coincidence. Maybe it was a drought year, that summer the garden was eaten. We did have two dry summers about that time.

This evening, the tenth night after the blizzard began, I sit at the desk in this small front room with electric lights on for the first time in more than a week. I feel their glare, the moonlight of the ridge a world away. Yet I will enjoy an easy bath tonight, heated by electricity. Still, I choose to go upstairs, after the warm bath, to an unheated, moonlit bedroom.

With the phone and radio back on, I have learned that most of western North Carolina and parts of Virginia and Tennessee have been without power or phone. The storm is called the Blizzard of '93.

A lot of friends and other people had, like me, walked out of mountain hollows for the first time in ten days to hear Irish music at the Pine last night. It felt as though we were wired together with the current turned up too high. The crowd couldn't stop talking, and I didn't hear the music as well as I wanted and kept hoping everyone would settle down and be quiet. It was Will playing Irish whistle and his sister on the fiddle and singing, both excellent musicians I had looked forward to hearing.

I especially like the sound of flute and whistle and asked Will afterwards if the smaller whistle were hard to learn.

"Easiest instrument there is," he said. "Here, I have an extra D whistle. Take it and practice scales and how to get the sound of two octaves out of six holes. You blow into the mouth piece like this, he showed me, to raise the octave. And we'll play together sometime."

Sitting by the stove in the rocking chair this past hour, I've been trying to do what he showed me and sound unbelievably bad. I don't think I will be playing with Will any time soon, but I appreciate the whistle and will practice.

I didn't try it when I got home last night after midnight, for an unsettling thing happened on the way. I had driven back to the end of the state road and parked the Jeep where I often do and walked the unmaintained road onto the high ridge of the farm, which faces south and is sunnier during the day. Falling night temperatures had refrozen large patches of snow on the road bed, so walking was difficult. With a small bag of groceries in each arm, I went slowly and carefully to keep my feet from slipping out from under me on the ice and was intent on that.

Suddenly, a light appeared on the road right in front of me and moved directly into my eyes, so that I could not see who held the light. An alarm blinked in my head ! This is what my mother always warned me about, though I didn't quite believe what might be happening. I knew I couldn't run without sprawling on the ice and called out, "Elliot, is that you?" Though I knew my neighbor would never shine a light in my eyes.

"Who's that?" an unknown voice, a man's voice, said roughly. "I ain't a gonna hurt you," he added, but didn't move the light out of my eyes.

Why was he saying that, if it wasn't on his mind that he could hurt me! Why was he blinding me and not telling me who he was, or at least what he was doing on this land? "Are you coon hunting with Elliot," I demanded, hoping it was one of Elliot's buddies.

"Who's that," the stranger asked again, his voice suspicious and still rough. His lantern's beam still kept me from seeing him.

Thinking fast, I bluffed. "Elliot's my neighbor and is going to meet me here at midnight when he finishes coon hunting," I said. Of course, he wasn't.

"I thought you must be hunting with him," I continued, and tried to look straight toward this intruder. The light from his lantern hurt my eyes.

He didn't take the excuse to be on this land, and his silence felt long before he moved the lantern. Then, I could see him several feet in front of me, a dark headed man, medium height and wiry build, with dark beard. I tried to act as if I really were expecting Elliot to appear at any moment, but I was scared.

The stranger was quiet for a space, and I could feel my heart thump, thump, thumping.

Then he spoke in a halting way, "I can't find the way out. My car is parked beside a road, and I can't find it in all this snow."

Hope rose, and I didn't ask him what was he doing this far from the road, though I wondered. I pointed the way I had come, for suddenly I remembered that I had seen another vehicle parked near where I left mine and had thought it someone at Elliot and Ruth's house.

"It's straight that way," I said, and didn't breathe as he walked, very slowly, close by me, trying to keep his footing on the ice.

There seemed another long stretch of time, so I'm sure I did breathe, as he made his way past me on the roadbed and continued out along the tracks I had made. I watched in the moon's light, not turning my back on him until he was well out of sight.

Then, the question rose in me, had there been someone else with him, still down the road ahead or in my unlocked house?

As I climbed over the split rail fence to take the short cut down the ridge, I thought how safe I had felt here and never locked the house, even at night. And how many times I had walked on this upper ridge, alone, in the middle of the night in winter, when no rattlesnakes or copperheads might consider it their place.

The snow on the open meadow was softer than the shaded and icy roadbed. And beautiful, so beautiful in the moon's stillness. I decided to enjoy this moment, each moment one by one, of the beauty stretched before me, whatever might come next. Deliberately, I walked onto the open white meadow. Deer track were all around though I saw no deer. I felt they were in the woods nearby, perhaps watching, a comfort.

Taking my time, holding to each silent moment, I walked down the ridge and rounded the damp curve. Thin smoke from the chimney of the house rose below and I felt a curious satisfaction, under the circumstances, that I have learned to bank a fire so not to come home to a cold house. The spring's moist air soothed me, and I continued down the familiar gap, careful not to slip on the downward, wet and dark path. Past apples trees and lower spring, across the dirt road bed still hidden under snow, and up the short hill to the house, I came to the lighted sun porch and pushed open the door. Deliberately, taking a slow breath, I stepped inside and locked the door behind me, something I have rarely done.

Taking quiet, even breaths, I moved from the small and windowed porch into the warmer kitchen and lowered window shades I was not used to closing in this secluded place. I looked in the curtained pantry under the stairs that go to the second floor and walked into the larger room beyond the kitchen. The wood heat stove was warm and comforting. I checked under the futon sofa before adding wood to the fire and doubled back into the small room in front of the kitchen. I pushed open the bathroom door in passing, then looked under the daybed and pulled down window shades over it and this desk. All was as usual.

Taking another deliberate breath, I opened the door to the front hall and entered that cold space, snapped on the light switch. Then, I walked up the narrow stairs, not pausing, choosing not to think. At the top, I slid open doors of the built-in hall cabinet, checked a tiny plank closet of the bedroom to the left and looked under that bed, and then under the single bed in the tiny front room. Finally, I walked into the larger east bedroom where I sleep and, in light spreading from the hall, for I want no bedroom light, glanced under the bed and into the curtained closet and pulled down window shades. Last of all, I opened the door of the dark storage space under the eaves and jerked the string on a bare bulb hanging from that low ceiling. The yellowed light showed everything as usual, and I felt the breath relax out of me.

It took a while to go to sleep. I lay in the dark, feeling closed in by shades drawn for the first time, and knew my feeling of safety on this place, my innocence or foolishness, had been breached. I do not want to give up lone night walks on the ridge or day walks into the wilder and more isolated parts of the farm, where someone could lurk without anyone knowing. Finally, I reached up and opened the shades, so that I could see stars and moonlight as I am used to. Then, my tiredness took hold and I slept. That was last night though, this evening, it feels unreal and long ago.

March 28th

Rob, my good friend from working in Raleigh days, called last night. He said to me, "You know don't you, Ella, not many men can drop what they are doing and come there to live."

I recognize that all too well. Yet, I also know this is my place, at least for now. Regardless of the cost, I must be here, no where else. It frightens me to think that if I stay here, I might live the remainder of my life alone. It is unimaginable that I could go the rest of my days without again feeling the touch of a man's strong fingers on my skin, his warm breath on my face, that oneness with another. At moments I feel that I will die, if I cannot reach out and touch someone with love.

But I don't die and am laughing at myself, as I write. My feet are sturdy stalks planted in this sweet soil. And my spirit settles into the quietness of the river like a migrating fowl, seeking food and rest. I would not, for anything, miss living here and want to meet each new day with expectation.

March 31st

Spring fell upon the farm within a couple of days after I walked back in across the ridge last Saturday night. Woods took on a reddish haze with maples budding, and suddenly there are a lot more birds in the yard, an amazing variety of them. Air has the feel of spring, yet shifts from cold to hot to cold from one time of day to the next. Evening light has begun to linger since the equinox passed. From this desk window, I have just watched the glow of dusk come through bare trees like a wash of palest blue over pencil drawing. Now the window has blacked out, and a distant star blinks above.

April

April 1st

April bloomed in fog, gold with sunrise. I saw a cardinal light on forsythia, its gold intensified by the citron air and red bird. Mountains jut dark blue above fields that greened overnight, and blood root blooms white along the bottom of the ridge across from this window. Each day, I watch for rare pink trillium to flower on a wooded rise where brook skips to river. Am eating winter cress that flourishes on the bottom land and its freshness makes bean soup taste even better. Am planting lots of onions, for the ones I grew last year did well, and I use onions daily. Hope to get early potatoes in the ground next week.

Evenings are damp and chilly and the fire in the wood stove, with kettle steaming, feels good. I will steep a cup of herb tea and linger in the rocking chair before bed.

April 4th

After walking the upper pasture this afternoon, I climbed the north facing ridge above the river, and was making my way through rhododendron and hemlock when I heard a loud, near snort behind me. The sound was strong and close, an animal sound, not a human one. Bear, I thought and was ready to blend into the surrounding trees and quietly leave him or her be. But, curious, I glanced behind me and saw a huge deer whose tracks it must be that I have watched all winter, large inverted Vs in undisturbed snow or soft earth beside the river.

For an instant, the buck stood, magnificent with his rack of antlers against the racks of tree branches, before his strong hooves crashed down through woods that face this house, and he disappeared. I like knowing he is near.

April 10th

Morning fog was smoke among trees, as though countless fires were warming tall branches overhead to hurry budding leaves. Then, in the afternoon, light snow surprised wild cherry blossoms, themselves like snow on tree branches along the wood's edge. I haven't planted potatoes yet, but have practiced on Will's whistle and sound better though not much.

April 14th

Last night, I came in from preparing potato terraces too tired to eat and fell into the bathtub and went to sleep sitting up in hot water. Fortunately, the tub is not long enough to slip down and drown and, when the water got cold, I woke up abruptly.

This morning, leaf buds were just before bursting from trees and, by evening, the woods along the meadow took on a green so sheer that it seemed imagined. At daybreak, a male cardinal had struck his feet against the bedroom window, as though announcing spring. Or something.

From this desk window, I watched a female cardinal come in afternoon sunshine to the male on a nearby shrub. In the heated light, I saw the richness of her feathers, deep red among soft brown. One has to be close to see it. Am reminded that I still have red glints in my brown hair.

April 16th

This afternoon, the day warmed enough that I dozed in the

hammock after planting potatoes. In what felt a dream, I heard a slight sound to my right and opened my eyes. The huge rack of a buck deer jutted through dense green branches of the spruce tree beside the hammock and almost touched me. I thought, I must be dreaming, as the large head pulled back.

Groggily, I closed my eyes and felt the soft brushing of spruce branches on my face. I opened my eyes to the deer's large and soft eyes only inches away and lay there without moving, still not believing. But I didn't want to startle him away, even in a dream. The buck withdrew his head.

Trying to wake up, I heard him move toward the house. I was still too surprised to get up and, suddenly, the deer's head poked back through the spruce branches again, withdrew again. I wondered what was happening and without sudden movement eased out of the hammock.

The buck leaped ahead toward the ridge across the road. I followed and had lost sight of him when I realized he was watching from trees at the bottom of the ridge. Then, he scrambled nimbly up a narrow deer trail and went out of sight, though I could hear him.

I climbed behind and, when I thought him completely gone, glimpsed the buck higher on the path where he had stopped as though waiting, rather than eluding me. I followed and he moved upward, still in sight. Just before the ridge top, the buck vanished. Just like that. He did not show himself again, nor did I hear further sound. I went on to the top and stood, perplexed, hoping to see or hear him and didn't. It was the north facing ridge across from this desk, between here and river. Was the buck just curious? Or what?

April 19th

The dog, or wolf, that I saw in that waking moment of dream, the day the blizzard began, is here. His name is Luke, and he is part wolf!

Carin had called day before yesterday to ask if I would

take him for a friend of hers, because Luke had attacked a young goat next door and could no longer stay there. The friend knew from Carin that, here, Luke would have space to run with no near neighbors.

On the phone a couple of weeks ago, she had mentioned this wolf/dog. At the time, I remembered my brief dream, yet didn't connect the possibilities. And Carin's friend, who found Luke badly injured further over in these mountains, had planned to keep him.

The veterinarian who treated Luke pointed out marks that show him to be part gray wolf, at least one fourth and maybe half. The marking of black hairs in his full tail is one sign and also the shape of his up tilted eyes, the vet had said. Luke's back legs are not quite long enough to be full wolf, he thought, though the legs are certainly long and Luke runs like the wind.

Already, he seems to have a sense of this property's bounds, I hope. For I turned him loose, with me watching closely, after one very long walk on leash around the boundaries. Luke marked the entire perimeter of this place as we walked it. How he did not run out of pee, I can't figure and hope it means he considers this his territory now. And will stay within it.

I do not want anything to happen to him, yet don't want to bind his spirit by confining him more than necessary. Hopefully, the scent of deer will hold his attention on this land. Deer, at least the does and yearlings, seem to stay within this sanctuary of ample woods and meadows, the only land nearby with no hunting signs and a half mile or more of river frontage. The nearest farm, Elliot's, does not have goats. His cows and horses are too large, I would think, for a single wolf/dog to attack.

Luke's erect ears are black edged and black hairs run along the crest of his head and back. His coat looks light in color with striations of a darker, tawny color. His fur feels impenetrable, as though more than one layer. It is not like any dog's coat I've ever seen, nor are his eyes like a dog's. His chest is noticeably deep, and ridged. Most notable is Luke's independent air. Though he seems friendly, or at least not unfriendly, he has not asked for attention, refuses to eat dog food and confidently goes about his business which seems to be exploring and marking the land.

He was neutered during surgery for the broken leg and other injuries Carin's friend found him with, and that makes me sad. I couldn't have done it yet recognize that, otherwise, Luke would range too far for his own safety. Many people fear wolves, even part wolves I am learning, and claim the right to kill them to protect livestock. That could have been the circumstance leading to the injuries Luke was found with.

Both evenings before dusk, I have sat on the grass beside Luke and talked with him. After awhile he got up and we walked across the road to bushes. Then, with dignity and some hesitancy, he walked up the incline to the house with me and inside as far as the airy sun porch. With tick season in full force, it's just as well he does not come further into the house. Yet, if he were loose at night, he would probably follow the scent of nocturnal animals beyond this farm.

I made a bed of an old quilt for him on the wooden floor of the sun porch and, before I went upstairs last night, sat with him on the floor for some time. And will again this evening. Carin told me that Luke likes to have his stomach rubbed, and he does lie down and let out a breath when I run my hand over the soft skin of his belly. His breath is sweet, like a new puppy's though he is fully grown. Carin said that the vet estimated Luke's age as at least two.

Often, I see him glancing at me with what appears to be curiosity, yet he turns away if I look at him. I watch him with curiosity, too. Carin's friend emphasized that I must establish myself from the first as the alpha between us, so I will be in control. That doesn't feel right to me and I decided simply to treat Luke with the respect I feel, and he seems to treat me the same way. I don't know yet to what extent he is wolf and how much he is like a dog, though he does not seem like dogs I have known and loved. Carin told me Luke doesn't bark, and he hasn't.

April 20th

Between the lengthening day and knowing that Luke is
waiting for me to let him out, I get up quite early in the morning.
Luke trots out the sun porch door with plain anticipation of
whatever is ahead. He wore the same expression of interest when
he rode with me into town. He sat upright beside me in the Jeep and
looked intently out the windows. Even with his presence, the farm
remains a vibrant collage of birds, a variety of color and the sound
of spring, the feel of spring.

April 23rd

Luke killed a fawn yesterday. I felt it deeply, for I had pledged
this land as sanctuary. At the same time, I recognize that for a wolf
to kill for food is the natural order of things. And with predators
gone and no hunting on this farm, the deer have multiplied beyond
what is probably healthful for them. I have noticed their increase,
and here is a wolf/dog, a natural predator, that needs a place, too.

I have been increasingly concerned that Luke has not eaten
dog food since he came, though I bought the best quality I could
find. With only the tiny student refrigerator I just inherited, it's not
feasible for me to keep much raw meat on hand though I think he
needs it. I have cooked eggs for him, but hoped he would adjust to
dog food. He has continued to look well and energetic these few
days, though he hasn't eaten much.

When Luke killed the fawn, we were in a remote part of the
farm. For the first time since the day he arrived, I had put a leash
on him, tentatively, to see if he were willing. He apparently gets a
scent of other wildlife when we are walking together and takes off
in pursuit, out of sight, twice across the river. It concerned me for
him to swim across and disappear though, each time, he came back
reasonably quickly when I called.

So, yesterday afternoon when I wanted to walk the lonely path, I wished for Luke to stay with me. I squatted down, before I hooked the leash to his collar, and told him my intent, feeling that he would sense it. He seemed willing to take the leash, and we easily covered that very long trail along the curving river. Patiently, he trotted just ahead of me, rarely pulling against the lead. At the place where the path veers this side of the rock cliff that plummets to the water below, where the dirt path loops back toward this house, I turned him loose. Almost quicker than my eye could see, he was gone.

Immediately, I heard what sounded like a baby's quick cry and then a more alarmed and urgent cry.

I called Luke, and called again, and left the path to follow where he had disappeared into a thicket. He stood quietly over a brand new fawn, beautiful with its white spots, long eyelashes shading its eyes, the softness of skin and nose, its long delicate legs. Blood gushed from the fawn's throat, and I could see its breath ebb and then stop. "Oh, Luke," I cried out! "Oh, Luke."

Putting the leash back on him, I eased him away from the dead deer so that its mother would at least know what happened to her baby, rather than find it gone. Luke was reluctant to leave, but came with me. I felt torn apart inside, for I had made a promise of protection to the deer, and Luke had killed a fawn.

I don't know what I expected, yet wondered what it would be like for the mother to return from seeking food or water to find her newborn dead. An inherent risk that she may accept better than I, though I wonder.

Memory flooded me of Mc's birth during the Vietnam War and my realization that, someday, this child could be sent to war without him or me having any say. I sat and rocked him a long time after he had finished nursing, studying his sleeping face with the little smiles that come and go on a newborn, inhaling the boy scent of his skin. I pictured mothers who, throughout history, have given birth and given up their children to war.

Yet, the fawn's death seems different, somehow, and I saw

how skillfully and cleanly Luke had killed the animal and stood quietly over it as the fawn died. Luke killed for food, I'm sure, though I prevented his eating it, at least then. By the time we reached the house, I felt more accepting and sat with him a long time on the sun porch and rubbed his belly. I sensed that he was confused by my response to his hunting, that my feelings may matter to him, or at least puzzle him. I thought, not for the first time, life is not simple.

As I sat there on the plank floor with Luke, I noticed that his upper and lower eyelids are lined with black that is haunting. It feels right for him to be here, a part of this sanctuary, and I'll let him and the deer and other animals work out their arrangement of predator and preyed upon.

This morning, we were down at the garden in the river bottom when I saw Luke, across the field, cock his head to one side with attention to the ground. Suddenly, he leaped up in the air and came down with all four paws almost together and nose to the dirt. I wondered if he were catching field mice, for I've read that wolves eat them. Perhaps dogs do too.

April 28th

Three mornings ago, soon after I let Luke out, he returned with a freshly killed groundhog and brought it to the door. He acted as though he wanted me to see it. I was touched that he seemed to want to show me what he had brought home. Though it's still hard for me to see an animal killed, I said, "Good job, Luke."

He lay down in the grass and chewed on the groundhog leisurely. For a while, I sat across from him in the sun. He continued to gnaw his meat off-and-on that day and the next and the next. By this morning, the smell of it was rank. Tired of the odor close to the house and naively concerned that the aging meat might make him sick, I thoughtlessly took the remains from Luke and with a shovel buried them fairly deep, I thought.

He looked puzzled and promptly dug them up, his paws

flipping the dirt quite easily, as though we were playing a game. He continues to chew on the pieces of groundhog despite the smell and clinging earth. His bowl of dog food remains untouched, though I change it each day for freshness in case he wants it. Which, finally, I realize is ridiculous, so will stop.

My heart lifts each time I see Luke run across the ridges above the house. His long legs carry him like a flash. And with Luke, I feel free to walk the far reaches of the farm. Today, he swam the river while I worked the garden, and he appeared to be onto the scent of something, probably deer, in the hemlocks on the far side. I called him back, and he was so intent on what had caught his attention that he seemed not even to hear me.

Concerned about his crossing to the farm on that side, though the cows are some distance over, I kept calling a loud yahoo that carries a distance. Soon, Luke appeared, surprisingly far upstream, and rose out of the water onto the bank of this farm. I was relieved to see him back on this land so quickly, and he trotted down to where I was with that interested expression on his face.

The feeling between us seems to be a friendly effort to understand each other. I find myself spending a lot of each day watching him, and I see him studying me. Though he still turns away when I look at him. I am learning to be more courteous and turn my eyes away, too. The lines of him come together in an intriguing way, especially when he runs. But what is unforgettable are his eyes.

MAY

May 4th

Perhaps, I am reflecting the season, this spring that is apparent all around me. The birds, the deer, the plants, and I, too, have taken on new life. Even the black snakes are mating in the attic. I hear the sliding sound of them across the attic floor and in a little while the loud thump and then another loud thump as first one, then the other drops from a rafter. I remember other years when, during this first week of May, I would hear them overhead or see them in the wood shed intertwined from rafters.

Then one drops to the dirt floor, looking relaxed it seemed to me, and soon after the other. I always knock before going into the out buildings this time of year. Not for the snakes' sake, but mine. I don't want them accidentally dropping on my head.

May 9th

My friend, Susan, says that her sap rises each year at this time. I saw her at the Pine the other night when a pair of musicians from east Tennessee played, one on guitar and one on banjo. Their music sounded like a cross between blue grass and rock, new grass, they called it. Though my favorite is the traditional old time, the beat was wonderful, and I could surely feel my arisen sap.

Many nights, I have danced with the broom around the kitchen to tapes I play while doing dishes, but that is pretty lonely. I like it better to go sit on the sun porch floor beside Luke and visit with him. I think he likes it, too. And that he enjoys the freedom of living here on the farm, able to hunt his food though he seems not to need a lot to eat or to kill just to kill. He shows no interest in Carin's cats when he occasionally sees one, though they hump and spit at him.

Some days, I see Luke streak across the farm so fast that I wonder how he can stop. Yet he does, beautifully.

May 15th

The shivering owls are calling tonight, a hauntingly beautiful sound. Earlier from the high ridge and the angle where I stood, I saw the moon rise full above the mountains as the sun appeared to sink beside it. That seemed strange, somehow, yet is the way it looked. The evening air was soft, and I could see long distances, it felt, across the ridges. Light went from color to gray as I walked down the path to the house, past the cooler air of the spring. I like to begin and end each day on that high meadow, and Luke seems to like it too and usually gets back to the house a little later than I. But he comes.

Each morning before breakfast, we go up and, while Luke is off on his own adventure, I mow more of a path with an Austrian scythe. It has a straight wooden snath, rather than the long curved handle of an American scythe, and is easier for me to use. If I think about it, I get the foot work mixed up. Yet, when I am in the rhythm of mowing and not thinking, it feels easy and as though time has stopped. Then, I will be distracted by the view or the sound of an animal in the woods nearby and get out of step. This morning I heard a farmer from two ridges and the river over call his cows.

Luke was nearby and I could see him listening, too. I'll go sit with him before bed.

May 18th

From the upstairs window this morning, I saw a fascinating live clip of Luke as he buried the remains of one of his kills. Holding the bone or hunk of meat with his teeth, he flipped the dirt back with one front paw to make a hole under him, and I expected him to turn around to cover his treasure in the same way. Instead, he stepped back a bit, tucked his head under and used its broad top to push the dirt forward over whatever it was he buried. Then he leveled the dirt with his nose.

May 22nd

Carin was up for a couple of days, and the river is beginning to warm. She and Luke discovered a good swimming hole, probably the result of last year's flooding, on the far reach of the mostly shallow river. The bank beside this deeper pool has large, flat rocks where we could lie in the sun and slip into the water. Luke came and went from nearby woods. Later, in the cooler part of afternoon, Carin wanted to go fishing and Luke and I went along.

Watching her brought back memories of my father, her reddish hair in sunlight, her intent interest in fishing that day, the river itself. I always liked to go fishing with him, but wasn't that much of a fisherman. I preferred to play with the worms or watch my daddy and Lemond fish, Lemond who was like a grandfather to me and my father's Cherokee fishing companion. I think they were kin.

One of my early memories is sitting on the large stones beside the river, a Cherokee woman grinding corn from small stones, with the largest rock my four or five year old hand could grip to smash the smaller ones. I felt, rather than saw, the shadow of my father's tall silhouette on the river bank and could hear the back and forth whir of the fly rod, as his wide wrist flipped the line into the secrets of the far side.

Rarely would his metal sinker catch the line under a rock, as Carin's did twice. She patiently worked it loose, refusing to cut the line, and I waited though I was ready to go long before she. Luke did go and was lying in the yard, eating on his most recent stash when we got back.

Carin had determined to catch enough fish for our supper

and did. I helped her clean the perch and brim on the darkening river bank, as I used to help my father after Lemond died. Carin and I took the fish back to the house to roll in cornmeal and cook in hot fat, good eating with new lettuce and spring onions. I remember Daddy and Lemond cleaning their usually large catch in the river at sundown. Water snakes waited to snatch fish heads, sometimes literally, out of their hands.

Supper would be late on the cabin's long screened porch that faced the river. We sat at a rectangular pine table that Lemond had made, now in this house. Kerosene light gave richness and shadow to the red checked oil cloth on it, and a night wall of screen wire pressed inward with sounds of frogs and insect calling.

Before going to bed, we would snake the mattresses, for the old cabin wasn't tight. I remember only once when Daddy found a black snake in one of the beds. I was relieved it wasn't my bed, though now I value black snakes a lot. And still remember a medium size one that followed me companionably around the farm, the first summer I was back here alone.

May 26th

This morning, I was in the kitchen when I heard such strident bird cries that I went to the sun porch door to see what was going on. Luke was no where in sight, but the male bluebird was flying around the bluebird house nailed to a fence post. A black snake's tail hung out of the entrance hole which was about the size of the snake. I went out and grabbed the strong, muscular tail and tried to pull the snake out of the birdhouse, but it did not budge. Probably, it was already full of nesting birds and too full to come back through the hole. Or maybe I just wasn't as strong as the black snake.

From inside the kitchen again, I heard another commotion of bird calls and went back out. A whole menagerie of birds, several different kinds, had joined the male bluebird in flying around the bird house, darting at the black tail still dangling out of it. I was amazed at this show of concern and helpfulness on the part of other birds that were not even the same kind as the ones in distress.

Later, the birds gone, the snake's tail disappeared and its head took position in the birdhouse entrance. The black snake stayed that way the rest of the day, probably waiting until its dinner digested. I had not been able to make out if the female bluebird were among the many birds helping the male, or if she were in the bird house with the babies and eaten, too. I haven't seen her and wonder where the male went when he saw it was over. What was it like for him to loose home and family so suddenly?

Rob brought this bluebird house he had made when he came up over Christmas, and I was excited to see the pair nesting in it. I will miss their company and color, their nearness to the kitchen garden and eating bugs. From now on, I shall think of birds in a different way, seeing how they rallied to help another one, their obvious community though diverse.

May 28th

Luke howled last night. For a minute or two, I didn't recognize what it was, for I'd never heard a real howl. I had left him outside later than usual while busy in the kitchen, and the moon came up somewhere around full. Luke's howl was deep as though it came from his gut, not just his throat, and the sound was musical though different from anything I've ever heard. I stopped still. When I realized it was Luke, I walked to the sun porch door and by the moon's light saw him further over in the yard, head back as he howled again. He didn't move to come toward me when I opened the door and sat on the porch steps without speaking, not wanting to interrupt him. Luke howled a third time to something in the distance or in his memory, I wish I knew. The sound of him stirred something deep in me.

May 31st

Have been asked by a western N.C. conservation journal, that published something I wrote a few years ago, to do an article on a horse logger in the next county over. When I called him yesterday, he invited me out to his farm and I went. Since logging with horses does not damage the forest the way large equipment and roads do, I am interested in it. And there seems to be a market now for such freelance articles.

The logger's name is Coleman Brown, and he is half Cherokee so we had things in common. Though I may be only half of half, and know little about it. Other than early memories, happy memories, of my father and Lemond and his family. I also have some memory of the woman who took care of me from birth until I was five.

A decade later, she came to see me in Charlotte when I was in my teens, several years after my mother had moved me there with her. I noticed then Catherine's high cheekbones and slender nose, the distinct shape of her mouth, her tall, graceful carriage and quiet manner. Recently, I came across a snapshot of her and saw clearly that she was Cherokee, probably kin to Lemond and or to my father. He was known to give work to kin, when possible, for the depression years were not far behind.

My memory of Catherine is that she always let me, as a small child, play outside by myself as much as I wanted. Which was most of the time, even if it were raining when she would put my galoshes on and remind me to take them off before I came back into the house. One day I had worn the wet boots inside and then thrown each boot in turn up to the ceiling, over and over, to make a path of footprints across the ceiling. When outside, I always knew Catherine was in the kitchen if I needed her, and that made me brave in my adventures.

This Coleman Brown and I strolled over his land in the early summer sunshine, with his pointing out different pasture grasses and weeds and their merits. And his telling me about horse logging, for he knows a lot and the horses looked strong and healthy. They are the

smaller Suffolks that he breeds and handles with much gentleness,
I noticed. Walking back to a handsome pole barn from his pond, I
was ahead on the narrow path through woods when Coleman spoke
behind me.

I liked your soft voice on the phone this morning, but had no
idea you would be so pretty, he said. By then, he was beside me with
his arm around my waist.

He had already revealed that his mother was fifteen when
he was born and other milestones of his life. As I managed to keep
walking on the path while turning to look him in the eye, I told him I
was the same age as his mother.

For a moment, he looked startled and then gave a little laugh
and said, "Honey, that doesn't scare me one bit."

Good for him, I thought. But it scares me, with a wild card
like Coleman. And also an article waiting that I really want to write.
I kept our focus on the story, and the beginning of it was already in
mind when I left to go home and start writing.

Later, from the high ridge here, I could see white mist rise
above the darker river as the sky beyond, and the purplish blue
mountains, took on soft oranges and lavenders. When Luke and I
got back down to the house, for he stayed with me on this walk, the
color in the sky was deeper. From the front porch swing, I watched
it go from color to gray, then black before a sliver of moon rose.
Though no more than a dash in the sky, it gave hints of light through
the huge oak tree that spreads over the far yard. Luke was lying
under it, his head on a paw, when I walked around to that side of the
house.

He was reluctant to go with me into the sun porch, and I sat
on the ground beside him and rubbed behind his ears. Which he
obviously likes.

"You and I are somewhat in the same boat, Luke," I said to
him. "In order to live in community with others, neither of us can be
as wild as we would like."

He rolled over on his back, legs straight up in the air for me
to rub his belly, his answer.

It was pitch dark when he got up and walked easily with me to the house. Eating some plain yogurt in the kitchen, a new luxury now that I have a pint sized refrigerator, much of the cream on top was stuck to the paper cover under the yogurt lid. I held this circle of cream by each side of the paper and took it to the sun porch and sat down beside Luke, who had chosen the cooler wood floor over his bed.

He sniffed, licked tentatively, and then licked the rest of the rich cream with obvious interest and a skillful tongue. His tongue was both rough and gentle as he licked my fingers along with the cream.

June

June 4th

Day before yesterday, Coleman called to say he had cut hay
and would be raking it with horses next morning. He suggested that
I come early to ride the horse drawn rake with him, and I did. To
the rake, he had attached an extra seat for two, and the quiet rhythm
of the rake's movement and warm company of the horses, as well
as Coleman, were magical. He was telling me about working the
Suffolks and logging with them and urged me to try guiding them.

But I sat there on the comfortably jiggling seat beside him,
spellbound by the quiet rhythm and feel of it all. How could we have
switched from such profound peacefulness to noisy tractors spewing
fumes?

I didn't want the raking to end, but Coleman completed it
mid day. We had just finished a quick lunch when two boys came
to help with getting up the windrows of cut grass. Coleman used
a tractor to bale the hay and that seemed inconsistent with raking it
with horses, until he reminded me that hay used to be stacked loose
in the field. Rather than bound and stored under cover, as he was
bailing his to put into the large pole barn that he built.

One of the boys drove a horse drawn wagon behind the
tractor's path, and the other boy and I followed on foot and heaved
the new bales up into the wagon. It was hard, hot work, but I got
the hang of it. As the wagon piled high with bales, the boy on top
had to help pull up the ones I lifted to him. Then, we hoisted them
from the wagon, several wagons full, into the tall loft of the barn, an
afternoon's work.

By early evening, the boys were stretched out on the grass,
saying they couldn't do anything more. I wanted to complete the job,
since there were not many bales left in the field. Coleman said, no, it

wasn't going to rain. He could finish up next day, it was time to quit.

He paid the boys as they left and walked over and put his hands on my shoulders.

"I'm going to cook dinner for you," he said. "But first, why don't you go into the house and shower off the itchy straw, and then I'll massage the kinks out of your back and shoulders."

"I'd like to swim in the pond," I told him honestly.

He gave the same startled look as when I told him I was the same age as his mother, then the same short laugh and said, "Okay, I'm up for a skinny dip."

"My bathing suit's in the Jeep. I brought it hoping to swim in your pond," I called back over my shoulder as I walked to the Jeep to put it on.

Coleman disappeared into his house and came out in bathing trunks, and we walked to the spring fed pond. On the plank pier going into the lake, I waited to see how and where he usually went in the water. He stood there, as though he had never been in it.

After a few minutes, I jumped in feet first since I didn't know how shallow the water might be.

Coleman gave an exuberant whoop, which he told me later was one of surprise and delight that I had jumped in first, and he dived in behind me. The water was warm in contrast to the cooling air, and we swam easily together as the moon rose. After a while, we climbed out on the pier and walked back to his house in a star filled night.

He cooked while I changed, then helped in the kitchen a bit and wandered around his living room and looked at pictures of him and others working the horses. Supper was good and I ate leisurely. Coleman finished before I, pulled back a little from the table and started talking vaguely about not having much time left. And that he couldn't tell me the circumstances.

I was getting sleepy by then, couldn't make out what he was talking about and wondered if he were trying to tell me he had a terminal illness. As I finished eating, he suddenly was out of his seat and lifted me out of mine and pulled me to him and kissed me. I was surprised by the strong rush of feeling I felt for him.

The telephone rang just then from the next room, though we both ignored it as we kissed again. Then the answering machine blared, and a man's voice started talking about one of the mares Coleman had left in Tennessee, where he is doing some logging.

"Oh shit," Coleman said, and went to the phone.

By the time he came back into the kitchen, I had collected myself and my belongings and told him a firm good night. And that it had been a really wonderful day.

This morning he came here, unexpectedly, and said he wanted to see this land, talk more about the article, and apologize for having acted like a sailor about to jump port, so he put it. And, he continued, he wanted to tell me the truth. He is awaiting trial later in the summer on charges of possession of marijuana with intent to sell. He expects to go to prison for a year.

I can't imagine Coleman imprisoned and feel for anything or anyone caged. It is well his phone rang when it did last night. I did agree to feed his stallion next week, while Coleman is in Tennessee finishing the logging job. Maybe, that's why he came over, to ask me to feed the stallion.

He also wanted to meet Luke, he said, and what he has told me about horse logging and sustainable harvest will make a good article.

June 6th

The ridge is especially beautiful with the lit, soft orange of wild azalea, called honeysuckle by local people. Mountain laurel, spoken of as ivy, is flowering its soft pink among the honeysuckle's luminous orange, and a larger native rhododendron, with its waxy white flowers and dark rose centers will bloom within the month, before the ivy is done. This rhododendron, confusingly called laurel, is already beginning to bud and will open its lustrous flower heads across from this window, all along the north face of the ridge, the ridge of dream that runs above the dirt roadbed between house and river.

Day light tasks of the farm keep me busy with practical necessities. The pump broke, so I did a lot of hauling of water for two days, then was able to get both it and the toilet fixed now that the roadbed has dried enough for a plumber to drive it. Bathing in the river brings back childhood memories of Ivory soap floating on the current. I swim in the icy water almost every day now. Bringing in daily wood for the cook stove and finding more to renew the pile has become a rhythm. There is plenty of wood down over the place, and I cut thinner pieces with a Japanese hand saw.

June 11th

Feeding Coleman's stallion is something new, for I've never been around a stallion. Or been responsible to feed any horse, though I rode a fair amount when growing up in Charlotte. And, as a younger child, happily bounced behind my father on the work horse, Bill, as we trotted along dirt roads on occasional Sunday afternoons. During those early years when I lived here in the mountains, I was probably too young to take on much of the animals' care. Though I remember gathering eggs and doing other things to help. I felt I was helping and even tried to milk the cow.

Another of my initiatives was to dig a water hole for the ducks around the outside faucet. With much labor, I used a small sand bucket tin shovel to dig out the damp dirt, a hole big enough for several ducks to paddle around in when filled with water from the faucet. During hot summer days, I sat in the muddy water with the ducks and also swam in the shallow parts of the rushing river. I figured out how to swim because I wanted to get to the other side of the river. And did.

I liked to run barefoot outdoors and jump into cow pies and feel them squish between my toes. Maybe that is why my mother decided to take me to the city to live. In August of the summer I was eight and a half, she took me to Charlotte to live with her. I wanted to stay with my father, the animals, the river, Lemond and his family further up the mountain, and didn't understand at all why my daddy let my mother take me away.

When I understood I did have to go, I went outside so that no one would see me fighting back tears and spent the afternoon with the dog I would have to leave. I remember singing, over and over, my own version of Carry me back to old Virginia, with the words changed to Carolina mountains. I wanted to stay right here, where I was.

Coleman had told me how to drop hay out of the barn loft, carry a bale to the pasture, open it and spread the loose hay inside the electric fence. The first day I went out, I saw that he had left a bale beside the fence, an easy beginning, and I spread it for Lightning. Then got a bucket of oats from the barn, as instructed, and started toward the center of the pasture to put them in a wooden feeding trough that Coleman had specified. Before I reached it, the strapping stallion left the hay strewn on the ground and galloped towards me so thunderously, that I almost fell over backwards to get out of his way.

Lightning stopped on a dime, just at my nose, nuzzled me with his warm nose, and went for the oats that I just managed to get into the trough. While he ate them, I filled a water bin at the fence line with a hose and stood and watched from that distance. After he ate, the horse trotted over to me and I rubbed his head.

Returning two days later which was the plan, I felt more trusting that Lightning would stop short of trampling me as I carried oats to the trough. Climbing the very high, straight ladder into the partially floored barn loft and pitching out that day's bale of hay was the risk. A misstep, and no one would have known until Coleman returned. I was glad that Luke was not waiting for me in the hot Jeep, though he was up on the sun porch at home all afternoon. It had taken a while for him to come willingly inside, so I had been later driving to Coleman's.

Luke and I took an extra long walk when I got home this evening. Though I am not swift enough to keep up with his runs ahead, he doubled back to where I was on the high meadow. We came down the path by the springs together, with him just ahead of me and the western sky before us, intense with color.

June 13th

Last night, I went into town for the old time music and ended up on the dance floor. Hesitantly at first, I joined in the flat foot dancing without partners and then one of the men asked me to jitterbug to the traditional reel music. It worked, and it felt good to be dancing and out with other people. I'm becoming inbred being alone so much.

Later, outside and back of the general store that had cleared a small dance floor inside, musicians were jamming up and down the alley. They were playing both hard driving and softer traditional music. Some very good fiddle and banjo players were there from the surrounding area. As I listened, the haunting sound of fiddle in these mountains, years ago, came back to me. When one fiddler played "You are My Sunshine," the slow way, the way my father used to sing it to me, I walked to the darker side of the alley. For I didn't want anyone to see the tears that salted my mouth and dropped off my chin.

It was a beautiful night with a high moon. I came home too restless to sleep and took Luke out in the yard, since he had been on the sun porch since late afternoon. After we came back in and he dozed on the sun porch, I danced a waltz around the kitchen, wishing like everything there were strong arms around me, my hands feeling hot skin and the shape of a man's fingers on mine. Finally, I wore myself out and went to bed and watched through the windows as the moon came in and out of clouds.

June 15th

On the third and last trip out to feed Coleman's stallion, the electric fence was down and Lightning was not in sight. I stood there, feeling a little frantic and wondering what to do when I saw him trot across a far pasture towards me. I waited and, when a few minutes later he again stopped at my nose, I reached up and gripped his halter and felt the silkiness of his mouth against the back of my hand. Talking, almost humming to him and thinking prayers, I led him, or he led me, to a small paddock off the barn. He went in as if it were his idea all along, and I closed the gate and set about to get food and drag over a hose to clean a large tub for water.

Coleman called this afternoon when he got home. Deer sometimes tangle in the electric fence and tear it down, he said. Lightning was fine in the paddock where I had left him. Where he chose to go, I said.

Coleman also told me that several of his close friends would be at his trial in September, and he asked me to come. I will go.

June 19th

The pattern of stars outside my southeast bedroom windows this time of year is becoming familiar again, like the stir of wind and subtle noises of this old house. Each evening, I sit on the sun porch floor and visit with Luke, as I will in a few minutes. During the day, I see him run across the ridges, busy with his life, an unforgettable sight. During the afternoon, I know where to find him under his favorite shade bush. After supper we walk together, and he ends up running ahead, and returns here a little later and before dark. With me always thankful to see him home.

June 23rd

Wild roses bloom and, through the open window directly in front of my desk, I can smell sweet air that lulls like sunshine on my back. Today is what I think of as a June day. The world feels expansive and looks lighted up. Elliot cut hay on the upper meadows this morning, after we checked high grass for fawns. We didn't expect to find any newborns this late in the season, but I wanted to be sure.

I remember a couple of years ago coming upon a tiny deer when I was walking, and it got up on long legs, so beautifully shaped, and tried to come to me. Though I was close, I may have been upwind where the baby could not smell I was not its mama. I wanted to take the fawn in my arms, yet backed away. It may not have been necessary that I keep my scent off of it, but I didn't know. A little later, I checked to make sure the mother got back for the fawn, and she had.

June 28th

As far as I know, Luke has killed no more deer. He brings his kills of groundhog and other small wildlife for me to see, and I am surprised how little food it seems to take to sustain his vigorous running over the ridges each day. As I write, it occurs to me that Luke may have recognized early on that it was best not to show me some things.

There is much about Luke, I wish he could tell me. An acquaintance related news of a female wolf/dog that sounds similar to Luke, found in this same range of mountains, further over, about the time that Luke was. I know that, a few years ago, gray wolves were being kept for educational purposes further northwest, over the Tennessee border near Knoxville. At the time, I met one of the men involved in the project and remember his saying they were careful not let any of the wolves get loose. They knew the concern that many people have about them.

Yet, one wouldn't have to be loose long to beget a litter with a local dog! I've read that wolves do not naturally mate with dogs. Why would they in the wild with other wolves? If unnaturally penned up all the time and one managed to get out, the usual pattern might be disrupted since there are no longer many wolves running around here.

July

July 1st

Morning always seems a fresh beginning, full of dew and possibilities, and I awake at dawn, eager to see the sun seep over eastern mountains. Grass is wet in early morning, and I got myself a pair of knee high green rubber Wellies that stand at attention inside the sun porch door, ready to walk up the high meadow. I've also taken to wearing slender leather boots that tie, ankle high, whenever I go off farm. To arrive at any place, I walk through dust or mud or rain puddles just to get to the Jeep, even when parked near the house on the old roadbed. And usually make a stop at the county trash bins on the way to wherever I'm going. Dumpsters are somehow always surrounded by mud regardless of weather, and I find it hard enough to arrive anywhere with a clean skirt, much less feet.

Luke seems to know, even before I myself do, when I am going somewhere and stands by, ready. He makes a graceful and easy leap into the front passenger's seat of the Jeep, sits alert and notices everything, quietly. He has never barked. His interest in what passes the windows, between here and town, is so intent that you would think he'd never seen it. Though he may have seen it just yesterday.

July 9th

I forget each year, until the ridge is again covered with their blossoms, how softly beautiful the native rhododendron are. They look like heaven, yet their low and intertwined branches are hell to crawl through, I learned years ago. Hence the common name of these sometimes huge evergreen shrubs that can cover an area, rhododendron hells. The ridge facing the house, between here and river, shines with their blush blossoms and dark, dark satiny leaves.

From the window here at the desk, I can see the flowers that look moon lit against the dark background, though it is barely twilight.

This angle of the ridge, framed by the window, brings back that fleeting dream of a wolf, or wolf/dog, standing on such a place. Now, I can't imagine Luke not here.

The gardens are doing well. Tending them, going into the river, cooking on the wood stove, writing, walking with Luke each morning and evening, make a good day.

July 14th

Yesterday, to keep my free lance momentum going, I interviewed a man who started an organization that accepts and safeguards development rights to farms. A conservation easement, it's called, means that land can not be subdivided or developed and will remain available as agricultural or green land forever, supposedly. Title to the land, and right to live on it and use it, stay with the owner and transfer with sale or inheritance. I am interested both in writing the article about easements and in the possibilities for this farm.

So called ownership of land is the responsibility that I do or don't take to preserve it for coming generations. And I don't want my future grandchildren, or anyone's children, to eat plastic food because we have paved over all the farmland and forest. Or worse, for their spirit to be hungry for a more natural world.

It was fun to talk with this man who has worked all over and will be in Africa this winter. Steve said that he periodically goes back to Lesotho, a very small country surrounded by South Africa, to amend his efforts there years ago as a young peace corps worker. He and his wife earnestly took modern agriculture practices to a mountain village that had a traditional system of agriculture, he gradually learned, better than what he had brought. He had the good sense to learn from them and now is an advocate for a local leader who has revived and enhanced the community's traditional methods. The local leader's name is pronounced Machebani, though I'm not sure of the spelling.

We had a lively conversation about whether humans matter to the rest of creation. It interests me in regard to Luke. Steve and I agreed that all life has intrinsic value, regardless of human perception. What I don't know is, does it enrich or diminish an animal's life, Luke's life, to be known by people, by me?

If I understood Steve correctly, he believes evolution is random. And that humans are bad news for animals. I feel that humans and all beings have a potential that has been present from the beginning, though most of us haven't gotten there yet. At times and places in history, humans have had a cooperative relationship with wildlife, perhaps initiated by the wildlife, that appears to have enhanced the lives of both by the knowing of each other. This question interests me, this possibility, this hope.

I know Luke adds to my life and I would let him choose, if he could return to the wild. There is no longer much wild, even if Luke were. I feel my way in regard to what might give him opportunity to be who he is, to the extent possible. And feel my way in being who I am. These wonderings bring back thoughts of my father, of Lemond. The way each of them, both of them, seemed to see the world, their "at homeness" in it. Strong moorings, fog covered, that hold me to myself and to this place.

July 24th

It feels as though the breath has been knocked out of me and is not quite back. For several days, it rained and was muggy hot. The grass around the house grew like crazy, and I got behind on the paths that I mow with the scythe. This morning, I was outside trying to catch up a bit on them when Elliot drove down the roadbed on his tractor. He asked, why didn't I let him do that for me? That he had the bush hog on his tractor and it wouldn't take but a few minutes.

I thought, why not? Then I'll keep paths open with the scythe, which is what I want to do. I like using it and want to let the wildflowers grow in back, as well as encourage native flora on the rise between roadbed and house.

"Just the paths, please," I said to Elliot and thanked him.

He nodded and did that at first. Sitting on the sun porch steps, watching, I was thinking that he was doing in a few minutes what would take me much longer with the scythe. In spite of the strong gasoline fumes and my recent reflections on the hay rake about peace and quiet, I was impressed with how fast a bushhog could mow paths.

Suddenly, when Elliot got to the rise behind the house where the wild flowers were thickest, he started mowing the whole area. Before I quite realized what was happening or could stop him above the noise and hot fumes of the tractor, the beautiful yarrow, milkweed, orange butterfly weed, and other flowers that had been a tangle of color were strewn over the ground. I saw that a tractor is not the right tool for a small space, and the loss of these flowers feels large to me.

"You were inviting copperheads," Elliot eyed me sternly, "too near your house."

I think he's right about that, yet Luke is here.

Still 1993

August 2nd

In the midst of things that require attention, I am savoring the quiet of summer's near end, the river, the garden's bounty and Luke, especially Luke. This week, I also decided a hard matter, and it brought home to me that I make such decisions alone. A national tree company offered me $10,000 for a thousand medium sized live white pines that they would dig and ball. The hard part of the decision is that the trees, planted on a ridge behind the house for Christmas trees and never harvested, are growing up too close together. If they are not thinned, they will not even make a good stand of woods, I'm told, and I don't know what to do about it.

Ten thousand dollars would more than repair this old house and pay future years of property taxes. Yet, I am unwilling to sell off a thousand huge balls of soil, or even half a thousand, to thin the trees. Such loss of soil could devastate the ridge. So I said, "No."

August 8th

From the double windows by the eating table in the kitchen, I look out on a hedge of white althea blossoms with crimson throats. Tiny ruby throated, iridescent green hummingbirds dart in and out of the flowers that, with their leaves, are the same colors as the birds, a feast for the soul.

Today, along with hummingbirds on the hedge, I saw a larger warbler perch on the nearby crab apple tree and please my eye further with its extension of yellow on the red fruit. For walls inside the kitchen are a mellowed yellow, with faded red checked oil cloth on the table by the windows and other touches of soft red in that north facing room.

A small cross stitch that Carin made when she was seven or eight hangs on the mid frame of the double window above the table. Its red, hand sewn stitches declare, "Love Make a family." She has wanted to add the missing 's' to Make and capitalize 'family' since she gave it to me for Mother's Day, years ago. I haven't let her touch it for it means so much to me as is, as does the box full of mementos and pictures of all four of my now grown children. All of them plan to be here Thanksgiving weekend, as they've been busy with their lives this summer.

August 14th

These ancient mountains are misty like the sea, their overlapping ridges and changing, shadowed colors, like waves. They rose from an ancient sea bed, scientists say, as do old creation stories of the Cherokee. I had learned in school that mountains in this area were not glacier carved, but upfolded. Now, there is some thought, I've heard, that these mountains could have been shaped by matter flung from outer space. Either way, scientific theory affirms the symbolism in Cherokee stories that predate western science. A favorite story of mine is the buzzard flying low over land that formed as a sea dried up.

When the buzzard got to this area, as I remember the story, he was so weary his wings struck the newly exposed earth repeatedly, down and up, over and over, and shaped these mountains. I like this image of a large buzzard flying in from a very long distance, his wings dipping and rising, as these mountains do, language that is descriptive and beautiful and symbolically true.

When Sarah, in her twenties, came home from seeing the Himalayas and then the Rockies, she said, "Mama, you've never seen real mountains."

"Oh, yes," I told her. These mountains, the Blue Ridge,

Appalachians, Smokies, for their names overlap, are among the oldest mountains on earth, scientists say. They've been gentled far longer than most mountains. And there are plants here, such as ginseng, found no where else except Asia. The variety of flora, evergreen and deciduous, has been well noted by botanists. Flowers and trees must like the moist air, as do I. And deer seem to like the light rain we've been having, for I see them daily on the meadows.

Luke comes into the sun porch damp on the surface, but water doesn't soak into his thick coat. I had been concerned that summer would be hard on him with such impenetrable fur, and he was noticeably inactive at the beginning of hotter weather. But, Kathy, the vet and my friend, says that his double coat actually gives Luke some protection, she feels, not only from fleas and ticks, but from heat as well as winter cold. He makes daytime cool places by digging himself body size bowls in the dirt beside shade bushes and dozing through the hot part of the day. Always at night the mountains cool down, and there is continuous fresh running water for him to drink. He continues his moderate and successful hunt for food.

August 20th

It has rained and rained and rained. Everything feels damp. But that seems a small thing in the face of the foolish thing I did yesterday and with Luke in the Jeep. We went to pick up goat's milk from friends who had told me by phone that, though the river along their road was swollen, the gravel road had only a little water on it in places.

If the river went over its banks, it would be several days or more before I could go. And knowing the four wheel drive and high bed of the Jeep can take some water, I decided to go while I could. Luke and I quickly hiked over the ridge to where I park in muddy weather, a walk for which he readily takes the leash in his eagerness to go along.

Driving on the state road was all right. So I started cautiously down the friends' gravel road to their house, the barely overflowing river running parallel to it on Luke's side, with him studying the water from his window vantage. We were doing fine until I went around an abrupt sharp turn. Immediately, the whole river, with trees and other debris in the turbulent water, seemed to come straight toward the truck. Instantly, I backed out of the flood water's path, unseating Luke, and backed further and turned around. As quickly as possible, we drove out the way we had come, water on the road getting steadily deeper, and the dark flooding river raging alongside us with large tree trunks like wildly racing canoes.

After sprawling on the seat and me when I backed so quickly, Luke calmly regained his upright position and was a steady presence. We somehow managed to get back to the state road and make our way home in the gray and unrelenting rain.

The river here flooded, too, and tore out more of the abandoned bridge built across it years ago when the old roadbed was a state maintained, not much traveled, gravel road. The high water receded quickly and did not reach potato terraces that are further back on the bottom land. It did bring back memories of more severe floods of the past, times when water would flow right under and somewhat through the old cabin that stood on locust posts within sight of the river.

August 30th

Yesterday, Luke was with me when I drove into town, and a ground hog ran out in front of the Jeep just after we got to the gravel road beyond the farm. He or she came out so suddenly, there was no way I could keep from hitting it. I felt, as well as heard, the thud and stopped, not wanting to leave an animal injured and suffering, yet not knowing what I could do. Until I got out of the Jeep and saw that the groundhog was dying and knew I wanted to keep watch with it.

In the ten or so minutes that I sat silently on the grass, I felt surprised by the groundhog's face. I had never really looked at groundhogs' faces or thought much about them, other than as ungainly animals that I usually see from the rear. I don't think I will forget the beauty in its peaceful dying.

Luke waited patiently on the front seat of the Jeep, his nose to the mostly opened window, yet made no effort to get out.

September

September 5th

I still wonder if knowing and being known matter, one way or the other, to the wildlife on the farm. Or more particularly to Luke. Or is it something he makes the best of as a circumstance of life? Or, perhaps, he or other animals are simply curious about when it happens. Maybe Luke would laugh at the question and wonder why I wasn't just catching joy as it flies, as Blake's poem so sings and soars.

When Luke flies across the ridge on his swift feet, the sight of him looks joyful. To watch him is joy to me, my heart soars! It satisfies something in me to know that he is part of things, and that I am too. One of countless, countless pieces of an unimaginably large whole, that we name Holy.

Does it matter to Luke, the deer on the meadow, the buck on the ridge, a bear that occasionally crosses the land, to know and be quietly known by others? To what extent, beyond human needs, does it matter to people to know and be known, really known, by each other; to know and be known by other species? Did, or did not, indigenous people, before they realized it could be their undoing, want to know and be known by other people who appeared from far away?

In thinking about what Steve told me of his Peace Corps experience with local, traditional agriculture in Africa, I am reminded that, by all accounts, the Cherokee and many native peoples had an amazing and documented agricultural system at the time of European contact. Archeological evidence indicates that some of the older village sites of the once huge, eastern Cherokee territory, centered in western North Carolina, had been in agricultural use for hundreds, maybe thousands of years.

Some of the settlers moving onto American land, repeatedly and for their own purposes, destroyed Cherokee fields, crops and orchards, though native people at various times and places had been generous in sharing food and knowledge. Instead of appreciating what they saw, could learn and had learned from American Indians, the new government of the United States arrogantly insisted on Cherokee adoption of an European system of agriculture that would side track women and tie down hunters. For the Cherokee nation to farm like Europeans was a precondition held up by the U.S. Government for its recognition of the Cherokee as "civilized" and deserving to stay on land they had occupied for centuries! These facts appall me.

Such governmental pressure began under George Washington and continued through other presidents, even Thomas Jefferson, information that disappoints me deeply. Andrew Jackson seemed especially determined to make the large Cherokee territory in the east available to European settlers. It burns me up to read of this, for it seems to me that the Cherokee and other American Indians were more "civilized," more wise, than many Europeans.

With traditional native agriculture the prerogative of women, though men helped with the heaviest work of preparing ground before they left for their summer job of hunting, Cherokee women, by all reports, had equal say in community life and everything that affected it. This equity gave them the wherewithal to see that every person in a village was taken care of, a natural tendency of grandmothers that was evidently recognized, valued and placed within the structure of clans and community.

Among the responsibilities of men, I read, were to provide meat, skins, implements and leadership to protect all in the community. Men and women worked together in cooperative ways to sustain life. Balance between masculine and feminine aspects of life was safeguarded.

History shows that many Europeans, not all, seem to have lost such balance before they ever arrived in America. Countless women had been burned at the stake, because they knew the medicinal plants! Destruction and imbalance still show in our linear, western society that fails to understand the circular connections of all life. Our loss is what indigenous people knew, practiced and could have contributed to the larger whole, if respected. And will yet, I feel. I hope.

September 12th

Have been in Chapel Hill, more than five hours from here, to talk with Rob. It occurred to me that his story of organizing local markets for small farmers in the southeast would make an interesting article. When I called him about the possibility, he suggested I come down to talk more and said that Sheila, our mutual friend from England, was in town visiting. I hadn't seen her in a couple of years. Rob suggested that I come the evening he was speaking at a Sierra Club meeting, and he would take Sheila and me to late supper afterwards.

Since it was just an overnight, I figured Luke would do all right in the enclosed and ventilated back of the Jeep where he could lie down. As always, he was eager to go with me and seemed to know before I showed any signs of preparation. The day before, he had sat beside the Jeep all afternoon, as though to make sure he went, too.

When we arrived at Rob's, rain was coming down in torrents, so I didn't spend the time catching up on his farm that I had hoped. Sheila was at his house and wanted to go in to Chapel Hill to a small dress shop, one that we had both liked, before going to the Sierra Club meeting. So, after walking Luke under a large umbrella, I drove her while Rob delivered his produce to restaurants, with plans for us to join him at the meeting. Luke rode in the back of the Jeep where he stayed, windows cracked, during the meeting.

Rob had told me how to find the church where he was giving the talk. Though I had not been there, I was familiar with the street for I had lived in Chapel Hill when working for the Conservation Council as a registered lobbyist at the legislature. Sheila is witty and fun, writes for the British Heart Journal, and was over here for a medical meeting. We laughed a lot, even before we got to the street where the church was said to be.

I had assured Rob that we would meet him there ahead of time, and we did arrive on the right street in good time. We drove its full length and the church was not there. We drove up and down the fairly long road again, no church, no sign that we could see though the rain had stopped. Finally, we saw a man walking with children and I asked him, Where was the Church of the Reclamation?

He looked puzzled and shook his head.

We drove up and down some more and hoped the church would materialize, for I was sure from conversation with Rob that we were on the right street. On the fourth pass or so, Sheila pointed to what looked like a large modern house and said, What is that?

At once, we both noticed the carved-in-wood sign that blended with trees, as did the unusual church building. The unobtrusive sign said Church of the Resurrection, not Church of the Reclamation. I evidently had reclamation in mind, since we were headed to a Sierra Club meeting. Sheila and I started to laugh.

As we hurried into the church, where we could hear from the door that Rob was already speaking, the funnier it seemed. The more we tried not to laugh, the more we did. It was embarrassing, because we couldn't stop laughing after we sat down in the not very large crowd. Both of us were shaking in the shoulders and making little hiccup like noises.

We were disturbing Rob's talk which I felt very badly about, but wasn't able to stop. I could see that he was getting distracted from the speaker's stand, and tickled himself. Finally, he paused in what he was saying and asked, "Would the ladies who had arrived late like to share what they found so funny?"

All Sheila or I could do was laugh some more and by then most of the audience were, fortunately, chuckling, too, as was Rob. He didn't seem to hold our rudeness against us, and we settled down to his very good talk about the importance of local agriculture. We continued over supper and, of course, I apologized to Rob for disrupting his talk. His face lit with a smile. "I've always liked to hear you laugh," he said.

Luke did well on the trip and seemed agreeable to staying in the Jeep, when we were not walking. He responds to people with quiet curiosity, is never forward. Neither is he backward. Both Rob and Sheila obviously liked him, and he showed a reserved and friendly interest in them.

September 17th

Coleman went to prison this week. I went to the trial and got home late that afternoon and let out a restless Luke. It was the longest time he's spent on the sun porch, other than the very long day that Coleman and I mowed hay. And one of the boys who helps me on the farm had taken Luke out on leash that afternoon. Today was surprisingly hot, though the porch has good cross ventilation with its two walls of windows opened.

The trial itself was not long, not long enough it seemed to me. But I had to drive to Asheville and then wait for the trial to begin, and afterwards I waited again with some hope of talking to Coleman. There are a few more things I wanted to check with him for the article. When I saw that wasn't going to happen, I left Asheville in slowed afternoon traffic and, clearing the congestion, still had a long drive home.

The trial was a farce. I don't like what I've seen of marijuana over the years and never tried it. But Coleman's trial was ridiculous, and I did not like what I saw of our justice system. Coleman pleaded guilty and asked for work release so that he could meet payments on his farm and child support, keep his fledgling logging business going, and admit himself to the county jail to spend every weekend for the term of his sentence.

The judge gave no sign that he spent any thought on what might be best for the community or Coleman, or that he, the judge, was even paying attention. During the whole trial, he appeared absorbed in reading something in front of him. No one seemed to listen to what Coleman said, as he represented himself, or even look at him, other than the four of us there who were his friends.

The district attorney went on a tirade about drugs that sounded as though he were running for election. The judge raised his head just long enough to give Coleman the sentence of a year in prison, starting right then. He was led from the room and taken off without opportunity for us to speak to him. I had the feeling that it was a done deal before trial and I did not like what I saw of our government.

That night of the trial, Luke stayed outside later since he was in so much of the day. Each time I checked on him, he was sitting in the yard in moonlight, and I squatted down beside him and visited with him several times before he was willing to come in. I hope that Luke feels free, though it seems necessary that he come into the sun porch at night. What, exactly, does it mean to be wild and what does it mean to be free?

September 22nd

Two stray dogs came into the yard today and ran, bristling, up to Luke as though trying to pick a fight. Luke stood with no apparent fear and looked at the two dogs with an expression of, what looked to me, disdain. I happened to see this from the sun porch door and watched the strays leave quickly with tails between their legs. I called out, "Good job, Luke."

He trotted over to the door and nosed me out and up the ridge path toward the high spring for a walk. We saw a deer, silhouetted on the meadow above, and I put my fingers in Luke's collar and he sat down on the grass beside me. We watched the doe graze, Luke's upright, pointed ears alert and moving slightly. Before we turned back down the path, a Red Tailed hawk circled wide in the sky overhead and swooped towards the woods with its raw call.

A letter came from Coleman with more information for the

article. Quotes from him are going to make it a good piece. He also wrote that he hoped to get on a road gang, so he can work outside the prison, that being inside with little exercise is the hardest part. He said the dead air is awful and the dead food, worse. But the guards are ok, and he is trying to make constructive use of his imprisonment and hope for early parole.

I remember hearing years ago of African Massai in Kenya who died, when jailed. That made sense to me and still does. Am relieved to hear that Coleman sounds well.

September 26th

A puzzle I've been thinking about in my reading about wolves, now that evenings inside are longer, is why European peoples, including both settlers to America and many present day descendants, fear wolves to the point of trying to eradicate them. And feel justified in doing so. What has been the fear in contrast to American Indians who, traditionally, lived in balance with wolves and other wildlife, forests and flora. What is it that makes this difference? It is more than whether one raises cattle or not.

Is it the difference between cooperation and competition? Is the prerequisite of cooperation, balance? Or is the prerequisite of balance, cooperation?

When I bend down to Luke, he greets me by pressing his snout against my lower cheek and flicking it with a neat tongue. I say, neat, because there is nothing drooling or sloppy about it. From my reading, the way wolves greet each other sounds similar. Perhaps dogs in a pack do the same; I've never had more than one at a time.

Luke seems very different to me from dogs I have known, dogs that I have loved. He has never tried to jump on me or anyone that I've seen, has never barked or asked for food or attention. There is a steadiness within him, as well as an independence, that is notable. Other than hunting food, he shows no aggression yet could defend himself if needed, I am certain. He is very strong. I feel that he would defend me, too, if there were reason.

The other night, I went out to dinner with a man I have known for years, though Luke had not seen him before; a friend who was passing through this area. He came inside for awhile to visit when he brought me home, and I noticed that Luke, in an unobtrusive way, managed to keep himself between the visitor and me.

September 30th

Grimes golden apples are in a basket beside the desk tonight, an old split oak basket with flat handle. Fruit on some of the ancient trees is ready to pick though hard to get to. I've been climbing on the stronger branches of apple trees, amidst yellow jackets, and leaning precariously from a rickety ladder to reach what I can. Before next year, I will get a long handled basket picker, for sure.

The river is quite cold now, I go in for quick swims, not yet ready to give it up for winter. Luke does not hesitate to paddle across river when he wants to get to the other side, yet does not go into the water with me as many dogs would. If he's nearby, he accompanies me down the shaded road to the river and sits briefly on the bank. Then, if I'm not out of the water shortly, he takes off for something up river or on the ridge. If he doesn't walk down with me in the first place, he will often appear after I'm in the water, wait a little while on the bank for me to come out, and pad up the dirt road with me to the house.

I keep seeing tree trunks cut by beaver. It is dawning on me how much wildlife there is on these ninety acres that I pledged as sanctuary. I had wondered if Luke's presence would diminish the wild life, but it seems not. If anything, I notice more.

October

Today, I drove down to Morganton where Lemond died in 1956 at the home of one of his daughters. I looked up his death certificate at the courthouse, for I have wanted to know more about this man whose memory is large and happy within me. I remember his silent footsteps through the cabin whenever he brought in water from the spring, the clink of dipper against tin bucket the only sound, if it were a metal dipper. Sometimes, it was gourd and quiet. And always the sound of Lemond's laughter, low pitched, tinkling, like bells ringing. Mostly, I remember the dance of firelight on his copper cheekbones that looked chiseled from rock, like that of the fireplace and chimney he had laid for my father's cabin. Lemond's warmth, his presence, his humor, were flickering fire.

One night I asked him, as he stooped before the fire grate to light a kerosene lantern for his night walk home from fishing with my father, across the narrow bridge then over the river and up the mountain. "Lemond," I said, "aren't you scared of rattlers?"

For rattlesnakes were legend in these mountains then. In recent years, I saw an old framed newspaper picture that affirmed the legends were not necessarily exaggerated. The photo was of a ten foot rattler shot near here a few years before I was born. It was round as the thigh of the large man who held it up to be photographed.

"Naw, I ken smell a sneck," Lemond answered, his eyes dark coals.

He was twelve years older, I discovered at the courthouse, than my father who was born in 1896, Lemond in 1884. I always assumed the two of them were the same age and recognized both as old enough to be my grandfathers. They were companionable friends, good fishermen both, though I expect my father learned much from Lemond. It was Lemond who had grown up here and knew the secrets of the place.

My father was born in north Georgia, not far away, just below the southwestern North Carolina line. That was where his mother had returned east from Indian Territory, after she was grown and married and before my father's birth. I've heard the story that my grandmother brought an old pair of Indian moccasins back with her when she came to Georgia. I think they had been her grandfather's. Her maternal grandparents had probably lived in north Georgia, a prime Cherokee area before the 1838 removal of southeastern Indians to western Indian Territory, now Oklahoma. The moccasins could have come back to the very place from which they had walked.

From Lemond's death certificate, I learned the names of his father and mother and from that could trace his grandparents. The big surprise was information about Lemond's paternal grandfather, Levi, who would have been a young man at the time of the 1838 forced removal of southeastern Indians. As I had entered the well regarded western North Carolina history room of the library in Marion, close to the continental divide, at one time a last stop before crossing over the mountains westward, the lady who oversees the collection asked what surname I was looking for.

When I told her Lemond's last name, and only that name, she replied immediately, "Oh yes, that family is known to have been among the Cherokees who hid out in the Gorge during Removal."

I hadn't said a word about Cherokees or their forced march to western Indian Territory. She was saying what I had known from childhood, yet had felt unsure of what I knew.

What I could not have imagined is that Lemond's paternal grandfather, Levi, whom earlier census records list as being in the North Carolina mountains long past the 1838 removal, shows up by 1870 to have left North Carolina for the same area of Kansas, the area that had been Cherokee Neutral Territory before and during the Civil War, at the very same time and place where my father's Cherokee mother was growing up!

I've never understood how she had ended up in Kansas after

the Civil War, rather than the western Cherokee area where she was born. Now I find that Lemond's paternal grandparents, deliberately it appears, went there, too. And stayed. This is surprise, a puzzle, and the more I think about it, amazing.

As I was leaving, the lady at the library desk remembered that a great granddaughter of Lemond's and another relative had been in the library the week before, searching for information about their family, and had left telephone numbers for other kin to call. Would I like the numbers? Oh, yes!

Am trying to gather my thoughts before I call. Both women live in other states, or I would leap in the Jeep and go to them to learn more about Lemond and his family, for I claim Lemond as family, too. In my heart.

October 8th

This morning there was hard frost, a surprising white shimmer of morning grass. I was more surprised, when I put a foot into a bedroom shoe, to find something bulky in the toe. Looking closely, I saw that it was full of orange split lentils. I went down to the pantry under the stairs where the large lard tins of dried beans and grains are stored. Sure enough, I'd left off the tight fitting lid of the tin of lentils I cooked for supper last night.

Throughout the day, I discovered the thin bright lentils in a jacket pocket, lentils in my pocketbook and lentils in other places I wouldn't have imagined. The mice, even with Luke's presence on the sun porch, are stashing away for coming cold weather. I am busy stashing fire wood, though not inside the house.

October 11th

Today, I picked up, quite literally, two successive Jeep loads of oak end pieces from the sawmill to use in the cook stove, along with branches I gather in the woods. Much of this new firewood and some of the already bought and delivered split hard wood logs for the larger heat stove, I stacked on the open, covered porch that extends across the front of the house, handy for blizzard days. I noticed that paint is peeling off the wood siding of the front of the house, that my home needs repairs.

The west end of the porch, where the old swing from the river cabin hangs, I left clear of wood. This evening, as I sat swinging, distant lightning flickered in warm twilight and Luke watched the swing's rhythmic motion from the porch floor. For moments, I was back on the porch of the old cabin, a midnight years ago. Come, the lightning lights the river, my father woke me to sit with him on the long screened porch and watch the river turn silver in explosions of light.

Canyons of brightness split the darkness that night, as thunder drummed ridges and vibrated with rain on the tin roof. Yet, it is the quietness there with him that stays with me. And the river, like a silver ribbon in the night.

October 15th

The boys from several farms over helped me dig potatoes today and spread them in the barn to dry before storage in the root cellar. Again, I noticed what I had thought coincidence the last time they were here. One or the other, or both, kept asking to go into the house. I don't mind their going in, but realized for sure today that they were making excuses to.

I like the boys and don't think they are casing the house, though the question did cross my mind. I decided that if they were, it was more reason to let them see that there is little of value that could be hocked. No television set or vacuum cleaner, only an old record player and broom, nothing worth stealing. Maybe, they are curious to see how someone else lives.

October 20th

Last night, I discovered I wasn't so alone as I thought, for during the night there was rustling near my bed. Enough moonlight seeped through the windows for me to see that my leather shoulder bag drooped on the floor in the direction of the noise, and two bright dark eyes peeked out of the top. A small mouse scrambled down the side of the bag and across the floor.

I hear one toe-walking in the walls of the house right now, a strangely lonely sound that brings back happy childhood memories. In the old cabin by the river, before my father bought this adjoining place when neighbors left for city jobs, I would go to sleep by kerosene lantern. Its yellowed light, in night breeze coming off the river, threw flickering shadows on the cabin's unfinished pine plank walls. There was no ceiling in the cabin, just beams and rafters bracing the high tin roof overhead. Contentedly, from the same iron bed I sleep in now, I watched mice play on beams above, as dark eyes peeked over and looked at me.

This afternoon, Luke and I walked the long path near where he killed the fawn last spring. Beavers have built a dam down river, just before the path turns this side of the wild cliff.

October 25th

Tonight there is a basket of dark buckwheat seed on the floor here beside the desk. I harvested the seed by hand, pulling clusters of hard, small triangles off with my fingers and curing them in the wide, shallow and tight basket. Today, I brought the basket in out of the damp of approaching rain and will grind seed as needed, and sift it somewhat, for winter pancakes.

Onions, dried on chicken wire stretched between rafters in the barn, are now in baskets under the stairs, a good crop. Before drying, I plaited several braids of onions and hung them in the ventilated sun porch, a handsome touch. Though Luke is the most handsome part of the sun porch.

October 28th

In town today, I saw the father of one of the boys who
helped me harvest potatoes. He asked if I weren't the lady Paul has
worked for recently. And went on to tell me that, though his son
usually doesn't say much, he had talked a lot about liking to work
here. He likes the way your house smells, the father said.

I must have looked surprised, for he explained, "The plants,
you know, the ones you hang upside down to dry in your house."

"Oh, yes, the herbs. Lavender, mint, thyme and the coriander
seed and sassafras root," I answered.

"So that's what it is. Paul said he and Jimmy kept going back
in your house because they liked the way it smelled."

I felt humbled by this revelation, that I hadn't thought of
such an explanation for the boys wanting to come inside. I'll invite
them in more from now on. Then I laughed, after parting from
Paul's father and crossing the street. For it flit through my mind
that the father may have wondered if I were growing and drying
marijuana, maybe the boys were wondering, too. When I first came
back here to live, some old timers thought my good crop of large
amaranth leaves, amaranth that I grew for grain, was marijuana. To
my surprise, they looked disappointed to find it wasn't!

November

November 4th

It took several calls to reach Lemond's descendant by phone. She is not as much younger than I, as expected. Probably Lemond's children got an early start on their families, as did Lemond. My father got a late start on his only child that I know of, me. I am the youngest of his mother's nineteen grandchildren, a generation younger than children of my father's brothers.

Lemond's great granddaughter, I think she is, had also been surprised to find census records that show her ancestors, Lemond's paternal grandparents, in Kansas following the Civil War of the 1860's. There seems to be no question that it were they. Why were they there? A mystery.

Mary told me other information in our conversation, including that Lemond's mother spoke only a language that none of her grandchildren understood. She communicated with them by sign language and she must have spoken Cherokee. It sounds as if Lemond knew the old language, though his children did not.

Then, I remembered that Lemond's wife, his children's mother, was not Cherokee that I know of, but half African American, half Caucasian. So it's not likely that she and Lemond would have spoken Cherokee to their children. I only learned in Morganton last month the family name of Lemond's wife. Her surname before marriage was the same as the family of a small plantation that used to be farther up river, not far from here. The father of Lemond's wife could have been born into slavery there.

She and Lemond lived across river from my father's cabin and up the mountain in a small community of cabins no longer standing. I remember Lemond's wife as a small woman, circled by grandchildren in their cabin.

The narrow dirt road to it was impassable most of the year, worse than the roadbed here which can also mire in mud and slide with ice. Lemond, a fishing guide, regularly walked down the mountain and over the bridge to our cabin and further, on to the lake after it was built in later years. I don't know if he had a car. My father, with his auburn hair and army experience during World War I, drove an old Studebaker to work in town. I can still picture that dark blue car, though I was young in those years.

Mary, Lemond's great granddaughter, told me she is still trying to figure out the mixed backgrounds of her ancestors, for her family had the story of a European back somewhere in Lemond's line, as well as Cherokee ancestors. I am trying to figure out, among other things, the mixed blood of my family, too. Mary and I will talk again.

November 8th

Last night, I read someone's observation about wolf/dogs that caught my attention. According to this opinion, it is not the percentage of wolf blood that determines whether a mixed pup looks or acts more like a wolf or a dog. It is the particular genes inherited. So, that in a litter with the same parents, one dog and one wolf, some puppies look or act more like wolves, some like dogs. Just as a family of children with the same parents can be quite different with their individual combinations of ancestral genetic material.

A pup of a litter that is one fourth wolf could have more wolf characteristics than one from a half and half parentage, the writer observed. If so, it would probably be true of people of mixed race.

I continue to wonder about the gray wolves raised for educational purposes in East Tennessee in the late 1980s. The more I think about it, the more likely it seems to me that one wolf got away long enough to beget a litter of half wolves. And maybe some of them then had pups that were one fourth. Luke could have been a result of one or the other.

Those responsible for the gray wolf project would not likely admit that a wolf broke out, even briefly, for to reintroduce wolves into wild areas is controversial enough, as is.

With cold weather I see Luke up on the ridges often, running like wind, tail out, legs long and fast. Then he comes home. I always feel a wild excitement to see him run like that; and later the warm glow of hearing him back at the sun porch door. Recently, he has begun to use his paw to rub a soft sound on the wooden bottom of the glass paned door to let me know he's back. His touch is gentle enough that the wood is unscratched.

November 13th

Today is the anniversary of my father's birth, three years short of a hundred years ago. I wasn't old enough before he died to realize the questions I wish I had asked. I don't know how to name, and I'm sure he wouldn't have tried to name, the intangible something he gave to me in addition to this place. More than anything, other than my children, I treasure what seeped, unspoken, from him and from Lemond. It had to do with the way of each of them in the world, their quiet pleasure in being simply a part of it, despite hardships, and their obvious respect for others.

When younger, they would fish all the way up river into the Gorge in their rubber waders, camping overnight. I've heard them happily reminisce about fish they caught and snakes they encountered. After the lake was built nearby and they got older, the two of them and often Lemond's son fished from a sturdy wooden row boat they kept there. It had a medium sized outboard motor on the back, I remember well, for sometimes they would take me with them on the lake. Sometimes Lemond's son, Joe, was with them, too.

We would eat Vienna sausage on saltine crackers for lunch, with an iced down Coca Cola. I never tired of looking at the blue mountains that ring the expansive lake, usually calm, sometimes stormy. And I liked the quiet presence of Joe who had been injured in World War II, I was told. He was never real well again, so I understood, though he was strapping looking, a handsome man. He and his wife had children, Lemond's grandchildren, not that much younger than I.

When my mother moved me to Charlotte, I kept trying to figure out the different world there. The strangeness was more than loss of family I loved, of river and mountains, and it wasn't that I was unhappy. For I really liked ballet lessons and spent hours dancing, outside or in my bedroom. And I was blessed to form a close friendship from the beginning with Elizabeth, who lived up the street. We were the same age and spent our days in the ranging woods behind our houses.

Elizabeth liked to play up in and among the trees as much as I, and she was braver in climbing them, for she had an older brother to learn from. I, too, liked to climb trees or sheds or anything, and both of us loved our dolls. When we were not in the woods, we played with our dolls at her house or mine. Yet, even Elizabeth thought in a different way than I, as did everyone in Charlotte, it seemed, and took for granted that I thought like them. Gradually, I knew I didn't and didn't know why.

November 18th

With the farm pretty much laid to rest, I've been catching up on house cleaning. To go with the clean house, I bought a mouse trap on my recent excursion to Morganton, one that doesn't hurt mice which you turn loose outside. The first night I put it out, there were two scared looking mice in the metal box-like trap next morning. I carried them to the woods, murmuring to them as I walked some distance from the house, that I was setting them free.

The next night, I wound the revolving door of the trap and again put it in the cool pantry space under the stairs before getting into the tub. As I soaked, I heard the trap door spring once, then again, earlier in the night than anticipated. Warm from the bath, I didn't want to go outside in the cold to release them. Nor want them to be frightened or thirsty all night, though I don't know if mice drink water. Before going up to bed, I put a jar top of it inside the trap and then, on impulse, cut a sweet potato and slipped half of it in, too. The mice were in good shape next morning when I toted them up the ridge.

The following night which was last night, before going upstairs, I heard the trap spring twice and again opened it, intending to put water and sweet potato inside. Two mice ran out into the kitchen and, as they ran, both turned back and looked at me. I am certain they were the same two mice, as the night before, and would bet money they were grinning! Luke, already asleep on the sun porch, seemed unconcerned about it all.

From now on, I think I will simply ask the mice to make their home elsewhere. I've heard that can work.

November 20th

Elliot asked if he wounded a deer that then ran onto this property, do I want him to track and kill it, rather than leave it hurt. I have a lot of respect for Elliot's hunting food for his family and know he does not abuse that or have trouble killing his quota on his own land. So I thought it a good question and agreed that he should not leave a deer with more than superficial injury, even if it ran over the boundary between the properties.

Yet, I hope there will not have to be shooting on this land, I don't like to hear guns even in the distance. And how does it sound to animals? The soft whir of an arrow makes more sense to me. When growing up during summers here at the old cabin, I learned to shoot a bow, as well as a rifle and a shotgun. Even then, I didn't like the sound or kick of guns. I enjoyed the bow and arrows, which I aimed at straw bales.

I wonder how Luke would react to the sound of a gun and if that is how he was injured. In the surprise of his sudden arrival, I didn't think to ask Carin if she knows. He shows no signs of injury now, other than obviously not wanting anyone too close to his left hip and leg.

November 30th

We saw beaver swim over Thanksgiving, and that lent magic to the weekend, as did Luke's presence. He obviously enjoyed having a pack around him, though people. And it was the first time that the three older of my children had seen him. The biggest excitement was announcements that in this coming year my first two grandchildren will arrive. Jena had told me earlier by phone. Sarah and her husband announced soon after arriving that they are expecting several weeks after Jena's baby is due, one in May, one in June.

After supper Thanksgiving night, Jena's husband suggested that we walk back to the river and watch beaver swim, for we had seen their dam and lodge on an afternoon walk. We set off with Luke on leash and a new battery lantern I'd put by for winter storms. When we got to the part of the river dammed by beavers, we waited silently in moonlight. Soon, we heard a quiet sound of swimming and switched on the lantern's beam over water, so we could see. About that time, there was a powerful slap of beaver tail.

"It's alerting others of our presence," someone whispered.

We saw first one, and then another beaver, move easily in the dark water. I felt awe struck by their gracefulness and keep remembering the sight and sounds of them. I want to go back on winter nights with Luke to see them swim. He watched the night river with his whole body alert, yet quiet and still.

As with the dying ground hog, I hadn't before thought beaver full of beauty and grace. They are, the river is their element.

It was fun to have my family here at one time though Lynn, a flight attendant, was on an out of country flight, and we missed her. Mc left Friday to join her, since husbands get some free plane time. Before taking off, he helped me close up things at the barn for winter. On the path back to the house afterwards, we remembered together weekends here when he was a boy and played Indian up on the ridge. Without my knowing, he would track me below and then surprise me.

As we laughed, I had turned back towards Mc when, suddenly, he reached with his long arm and pulled me in his direction. Though it is late November and chilly, a copperhead stretched in the sun on the path just ahead, the path we had walked over to the barn shortly before.

Sarah tells me that I hide in the kitchen when all of them are here. To me, it feels that I keep meals going and enjoy the sound of their voices in the next room, with Carin and Jena's southern accents getting more and more pronounced as they bounce off each other's. Sarah lost some of hers when she lived and worked on the west coast for awhile. As always, I miss them acutely when they leave though I am also tired by then. I'm not used to staying up late visiting.

The night before they left, with all in beds over the house, Jena called out good night to each one in the family by name, as she used to do when growing up, an endearing memory. A mother's heart is full of memories.

And the house seems to be full of hidden orange lentils. I found more of them when I took a pair of shoes that I hadn't worn lately, out of pockets of the shoe bag in my closet. And there were lentils in the living room futon sofa when we opened it for a bed. No telling how many caches are still hidden. Maybe Luke should be in the house, though I haven't seen or heard any mice in the past week or so.

December

This morning when I sat down to breakfast, I heard Luke's paw on the sun porch door, more strongly than usual. I had let him out earlier, so got up to let him in. It had turned surprisingly cold last night for this early in the winter but, instead of wanting to come in, Luke insistently nudged my hand with his nose. He obviously wanted me to come out. I grabbed a wind breaker and wool scarf hanging near the door to put over the wool sweater, slacks and socks I already had on. And slipped my feet into the green Wellies as I went out the door, almost but not quite enough clothes for the unexpectedly frigid temperature.

Luke had darted towards the ridge, and I saw him ahead of me on the path, seated upright, looking intently in the direction of Elliot's land. As I caught up with him, I heard the ripping noise of a chain saw in the distance and walked on, farther than I had meant to go in the sharp wind. I wanted to see what had caught Luke's attention, and he ran ahead.

Elliot was cutting firewood just over his line, and when he saw us called out, "Morning, are you out on your walk?"

I went nearer and he asked, "Have you seen the big buck lately, the one with fourteen points," I think he said.

We had never talked about the buck I saw earlier in the year, which I suppose had fourteen points on his very large rack. I hadn't counted and hedged now, for I didn't want a hunter to know of him.

Elliot continued, "I haven't seen him in the past two weeks and am afraid someone's shot him. I keep watching and hoped he was over your way."

My heart felt as though it slipped a bit, when Elliot said that. For since Thanksgiving, I had noticed the absence of the buck's large V shaped tracks near the river and wondered about him. I told Elliot about the tracks, though not about the buck's coming to the hammock last spring.

"I'm afraid someone got him," he said. "He's been around these woods a long time, and I never shot him even when I wanted fresh meat. A buck like that shouldn't be hunted, he was part of the place."

I was seeing a new dimension of Elliott and again wondered what the buck was doing when he led me up the ridge that day.

December 10th

Just returned from a night walk with Luke who, with his inflated coat and the snow's reflection, looked exactly like a winter photograph of a light colored gray wolf on a post card that a friend recently sent to me. Pausing in the roadbed, I noticed there were two holes in the snow clouds overhead and from one, a small circle southward, the crescent moon shone out of inky sky. Eastward, in a larger opening of clouds, were the lights of several stars. When I came in from the damp and windy cold, Luke continued to stand in whitish moonlight under the huge old oak tree, as though listening for something. It was clear he was not ready to come in and also clear that winter is his element. I will go back to him in a few minutes.

December 19th

Last week, I awoke with small icicles in my nose and realized that it was too cold to be sleeping with windows wide open beside me. Two days later, I found out what it is like to be sick a mile from anyone. It really wasn't that bad, thanks to a recently installed electric wall heater, set for minimum heat. I had it put between kitchen and bath to protect new plumbing on icy nights, though it would be of no use if electric lines were down. While sick, I stayed on the daybed in this small front room, here where the desk is, and slept quite warmly through most of three days and nights of fever and assorted aches.

What concerned me was Luke, though I did manage to let him out each morning and in at night. Each evening when I eased my way to the sun porch door, he was close by outside as though waiting. He came right in and I invited him all way into the house. When he chose not to come past the sun porch, I left the door into the kitchen slightly ajar so he could push it open. I think he prefers the colder sun porch.

Yesterday, I awoke a little shaky, but none the worse for wear. It felt luxurious to get the cook stove fire going again and sit close to it with a cup of steaming tea, and then poach eggs. And almost as sumptuous to take a bath with sprigs of lavender in the water and go weakly back to daybed and warm comforters to read.

I came across a quote from a talk that Kirkpatrick Sales had given somewhere. Essentially, he said that to know the earth we must know the place where we live, its soils, waters, winds, rhythms and fruits.

That is what people who live close to the land or water have always done. They become part of a particular place and the particular place is part of them, something many European settlers did not seem to understand about the Cherokee and other native peoples. Or, perhaps, about themselves.

December 31st

Carin came for Christmas and was here with Luke and me the day after, when Rob called. He was in Ohio on his way to the Indiana State Library, and his car had broken down. He thought it would be worth my while, he said, to drive up and take him on to Indianapolis while his car was repaired. So that I, too, could see the late 1800s census agricultural schedules that he sought.

I laughed at his tactic to hitch a ride and didn't feel much interest in old census records, but knew it would be fun to see Rob. And I remembered that my father's father, the one who had gone to Kansas and married my grandmother, had grown up in Indiana. Rob had tried before to interest me in genealogy, and suddenly I liked the idea of learning what I could.

Hearing my end of the conversation from the kitchen, Carin called out, "Go, Mama, go. I can stay a few days longer and take care of Luke."

So I made plans with Rob to pick him up in Cincinnati the next morning and hurried to put clothes and food in the Jeep and get started. A light snow had begun to fall, and I wanted to get out while I could. It had been dry and cold the preceding week, the roadbed hard, so the Jeep was parked near the house.

Carin helped me carry things to it, Luke trotting between us. I hugged her and stooped to tell Luke good bye, put my cheek against his nose and mouth. He licked me with quick, neat licks. "I'll be back, Luke," I said.

I felt he had learned what those words mean between us and then remembered, always before I had used them in the context of hours, not days. So I bent down again, close to him, and pictured four nights of dark in turn between stretches of daylight, hoping he would pick up my meaning, and repeated, I'll be back.

It was blowing snow all the way into Kentucky, not hard, and I stopped overnight in Berea and set my alarm to be off very early next morning. Rob was waiting in Cincinnati where he said he would be and got behind the wheel, and we kept going. We were in Indianapolis by lunch time and, still early in the afternoon, found that the agricultural schedules were not in the Indiana State Library. An old man, who worked there, told Rob he was quite sure they were in the Archives at Madison, on the Indiana side of the Ohio River across from Kentucky.

We drove hard and stopped again, and by late afternoon Rob had copies of the schedules he wanted. I had discovered interesting bits of information in the archives, information new to me about the Irish side of my father's family. By dark, we were driving out of

Indiana, crossed the bridge into Kentucky, and stopped for supper in a restaurant south of Louisville. After ordering, we scanned the agricultural schedules that Rob had gone to Indiana to get, and they were as fascinating as Rob said they would be. It would have been worth my while to drive up just to see them.

And even more to see and feel the Ohio, more beautiful than I had imagined an industrial river could be. Part of the late afternoon in Madison, I stood on its cold bank in the wind, taking in this river that my ancestors traveled by barge to Kentucky, I had just learned. From the western part of Pennsylvania, they had fought against the British in the American Revolution, for it had been the British who took their land on the north coast of Ireland and in the Hebrides Islands, just northeast of Ireland. I had known from family stories they had come from Co. Donegal, the northwestern and wild part of Ireland and settled in western Pennsylvania.

Before my hasty departure from home, I found and took with me a copy of names and dates from my paternal grandfather's Bible about these Irish ancestors. They had landed in Philadelphia in the mid seventeen hundreds, gone westward to the Mongahala River area, still Indian country, and eventually ended up in Kentucky. Now that Rob had the agricultural schedules in hand, he was intent on my finding more about my family and noticed that they, by the late 1790s, were in Elizabethtown where we were eating supper!

"The thing you need to do," he said over dinner, "is to look in the phone book here at the restaurant's pay phone when you finish eating. Look for your family's surnames and call those names until you find someone with the same ancestors, someone who knows something about them." He pulled quarters out of his pocket and handed them to me.

I really wanted just to sit over supper and visit with Rob, but he was so insistent that I finally got up and went to the pay phone. Thinking I would make two calls just to satisfy him, I hit jackpot on the second one. A woman who sounded older had answered the first call, why yes, those were her husband's ancestors. He'd passed on, and she didn't know that much about his family, but he had a cousin there in Elizabethtown who knew everything.

She gave me his number, and I made a third call. When Cousin Sam answered, I realized quickly that he did know and was a distant cousin of mine on my paternal grandfather's side. He invited me to come right over to talk more and, with Rob to go with me, I accepted. We stayed at Sam's quite late, trying to take in the torrent of research he had done on his ancestors, many of whom were also mine. More important were the family stories he had heard over and over from his mother and grandmother.

They meshed exactly with fragments of information I knew from my own family, pieces that I had not been able to put together. For my paternal grandmother was gone long before she could tell her grandchildren stories, before she could tell much to our fathers.

As the evening with Sam wound down, I asked just on a chance, did he knew anything about the family of my paternal grandmother, the Johnsons? Not that I had any idea my grandmother's people had been in Kentucky or that they, too, would be Sam's ancestors, as those of my father's father definitely were.

"You mean Tom Johnson," he asked, "the one whose mother was half Cherokee and half French?"

My ears stood straight up. Straight up!

Sam kept talking. About 1770, maybe 1775, Tom Johnson, whom Sam knew about from his Indian grandmother, had married a Cherokee woman on the border of western North Carolina and Tennessee. Tom's father, probably mostly Cherokee himself, had the surprising name of Alonso. Tom's mother, Sam said, was the daughter of a French girl who was raised by the Cherokee and had married a Cherokee.

In the mid 1790s, Tom, mostly Cherokee himself, and his Cherokee wife came from the North Carolina/Tennessee border by way of Ohio to Kentucky. One of their grown sons, Hugh Hyram, came with them. At least one other son, Abraham, stayed in the mountains of North Carolina.

Just recently, Cherokees descended from a relative of Tom Johnson's wife had come to Elizabethtown from the North Carolina mountains, Sam continued, to find cousins descended from her. Sam, as one of those descendants, had talked with them.

My ears stood up, first of all, because Tom Johnson was the name of my grandmother's oldest brother in the Cherokee Nation of Oklahoma, the one who kept up a correspondence with my father at least from the time his mother died until the end of this uncle's life. My father spoke of his Uncle Tom many times, and I could see that their ongoing exchange of letters had meant a lot to my daddy.

But that Tom Johnson, who would have been my great uncle, my grandmother's brother, lived during the last half of the 1800s and into the early 1900s, Sam was talking about a Tom Johnson of a century earlier. Yet all the things Sam told me meshed with what little I knew of my father's mother's family, and I am trying to put it together.

Before we left Elizabethtown the next day, Rob and I searched courthouse records and found an early 1800s plot map that showed, one or two generations before my paternal grandparents were born, two families with the same surnames as these grandparents on adjoining tracts of land. A third tract, adjacent to them, carried the same last name of Lemond's family! I am stunned and stunned.

The house feels silent with Carin gone and Luke may be missing her, too. I'll go sit with him before bed.

1994

A raccoon attacked Luke yesterday. It happened so fast and furiously that I am still trying to take it in. I had let Luke out early, as usual, and he soon come back into the sun porch which was not usual. About nine in the morning, we went out together to walk up the ridge to the Jeep. He was ahead of me as we came out of the house and, as he passed under the medium size maple tree about twenty five feet from the door, a raccoon jumped off a higher branch onto Luke's back.

Though I was right behind Luke, I could hardly see what happened next because the fight between them was so fierce. Once, the raccoon got away, went back up the tree and jumped right down on Luke again! I thought then that something was badly wrong. Though Luke is adept at killing smaller animals, it looked as though this one was going to kill him. The intense fight went on for a full hour, I later saw by the clock, with me standing in the snow, watching and helpless.

From its behavior, I suspected the raccoon was rabid and that, if I intervened, it would attack me. Also, I didn't want to distract Luke's concentration and felt that he could handle the situation better with me out of the way. But I couldn't leave Luke or take my eyes off of him. I stayed close and kept moving out of the way of their fight and saying prayers.

Finally, it ended in the icy stream that comes down from the springs. It looked as though the raccoon was drowning Luke, and I was frantically searching for some way to stop him, when Luke reared his full height out of the water. He came down on the raccoon, apparently with his teeth in its neck, and everything stopped. Luke dragged himself out of the brook with blood seeping from several wounds, including his nose. Tears of relief ran down my face, as I encouraged him back to the sun porch and onto his blanket. I knew to be careful how I touched him with the raccoon's saliva over him and in the dripping blood, for I had heard there was rabies in the county.

It was afternoon before I reached Kathy by phone, though I called her repeatedly. She was getting ready to leave the veterinary hospital after a day of surgery and, even with new snow falling, offered to meet us at the end of the state road if Luke and I could walk out. To drive over the ridge would have been too risky for her. She stressed that I must find a way to bring the dead raccoon out with me, without touching it, so that it could be tested. With a pitchfork, I got the frozen body out of the shallow stream and into a burlap sack which I carried over my shoulder with one gloved hand, and held a leash to Luke with the other. It was a mile long and hard walk for both of us, up over the ridge and out to the road, in snow and wind.

Kathy's car was waiting when we got to the state road and, with her usual efficient gentleness, she cleaned Luke's wounds, none of which needed stitches. She gave him another rabies shot though he was current, and said that she would take a booster vaccine herself, if the raccoon tested positive. Kathy wore gloves while handling Luke, as did I, but he had sneezed while she examined him, and she was more in the direction of the sneeze. I was holding him from behind. Luke's mouth had been in contact with the raccoon that Kathy thought would prove rabid. I keep repeating that, I guess, because I'm still trying to take it in.

Until I hear otherwise, Luke is quarantined and, if the test is positive, he will have to be kept up for at least three months. Kathy said she would vouch for me at the health department that I would quarantine him here at home, for neither of us can imagine Luke caged. It will be hard enough to keep him in the house. But he is alive. And he protected me, for without Luke, it might have been me the raccoon attacked. I couldn't have fought him like Luke.

January 15th

When I awoke early this morning to take Luke outside, I
couldn't tell at first if it were daylight or moonlit night. Then, out
of the eastern bedroom windows, I saw a tip of sun rising and from
a downstairs window discovered a shape of round moon still bright
in the western sky. Word came last night in a phone call from Kathy,
that the raccoon was rabid and Luke is quarantined for three months.
At least he will be free before summer.

Kathy went on to tell me that no one knows for sure if rabies
inoculations work on wolf hybrids. There is no indication that they
don't, she said, just no proof, yet, that they do. She recommends
that I take the series of rabies shots, just in case Luke becomes rabid.
Knowing it to be a hard series and my body's tendency to react very
badly to inoculations, I decided to trust my gut feeling and Luke,
to come through this himself and not to hurt me. In fact, I am
encouraging him to come into the house rather than stay so alone
on the sun porch though I think he likes the cold. I leave the door
between it and the kitchen partly open, so that he can come in if he
chooses. So far, he hasn't.

We spend a good part of the day walking, Luke on leash and
only on this property, which the quarantine stipulates. For me, it is
very cold to walk so early each morning and late each evening. After
dark, I am especially concerned about the possibility of other rabid
animals attacking us. I hear the epidemic in the county is quite bad,
with a raccoon biting some man on his front porch, and that even a
few cats and a horse have been infected. So I am vigilant during all
our walking and apprehensive after dark, as much as I like to be out
in winter night. I remember the beavers' swimming, and wish it felt
safe for Luke and me to walk that far to watch them.

I feel for him that he has to be dependent on me for three
months, unable to run since I'm not very fast, without wild meat
since I don't hunt, and confined to a house when he obviously loves
snow and cold days. Luke looks at me as though puzzled, when I

take him in and out on leash. Several times he has lain on the ground when we arrived back at the house from a walk and his face plainly says he doesn't want to come into the sun porch.

I do not try to force him or sweet talk him or make him feel badly that he is doing a sit down strike. Though eager to go inside and warm up, I squat down beside him and talk quietly about the situation we are in, feeling that he will get the essence of it.

Eventually, he gets up and walks ahead of me up the three steps and into the sun porch. His eyes look surprised that I ask that of him. And disappointed, then resigned. Yet, I sense a trust building between us.

We walk over a large part of the farm at least four times a day, for I see that he needs extensive walking and extended time outside. He does not trot outside and immediately do his business from one end of a leash with a cold human being attached to the other. He has a strong quality of dignity. So we are settling in for the long haul of a winter with constraints.

Am also doing editing for a local magazine and finished the article on farmland protection. The one on horse logging will be published in the spring. So I hope to make enough by year's end to pay property taxes which, fortunately, are not very much.

Walking with Luke, writing and tending the fire and daily pot of soup have a rhythm that I like. Now, for our walk before bed.

January 23rd

Sunrise this morning was a vermilion band above blue mountains, though the sun has not shown itself since. The weather radio called for rain, but in late morning when Luke and I were walking farther than usual from the house, snow suddenly pelted out of the sky. The flakes were so thick that it was hard to see ahead, and the ground was beginning to ice before we reached home. Snow was coming down so fast that Luke and I, both, were exhilarated by the time we reached the house, and I came inside wanting to tell someone about my pleasure in it. It is in such joyful moments that I most want to be with a mate, to share my happiness in this place. Rob has asked me if I get lonesome, and I told him, "It's the times I am most happy that I feel lonesome."

He has called a couple of times since our trip, and there is a bond between us, a recognition of something shared, that I appreciate. He is a decade younger than I and, more important, is that I want to be here in this place, this particular place, and his particular place is elsewhere. So I consider Rob among my favorite friends and enjoy his telephone calls, though they usually wake me up. He always phones after rates go down at eleven. Night person that he is and I, a day person, probably wouldn't do well together anyway.

The snow stopped in the afternoon, and the accumulation is not deep. Even so, the landscape is white with dark and grayed greens of rhododendron and hemlock. My chapped cheeks feel red. I smell the soup for supper, it always seems to be white bean on white snow days. It's fragrance reaches here to the desk, and I will go give it my attention. Luke is settling in, as am I, and I'm buying raw meat with bones for him to eat or, more exactly, bones with some raw meat on them. He is eating some dog food now.

January 29th

In the woods late this afternoon, we watched what may have been two Cooper's Hawks, for they were more slender than the Red Tails, and Luke noticed them, too. One, then the other, sailed into the top of a tall tree. There was the loud caw of crows, and the small sleek hawks left the tree and flew on. Then, we came upon two deer by the river, does, and stayed a distance, so not to interrupt them. I wished for Luke that he could run free and miss seeing that, yet enjoy his staying close on walks.

February

The events with Luke have diverted me from pulling together my notes from Sam about the family of my father's father and, it turned out, the family of my father's mother, too. It was my paternal grandfather's ancestors that I knew had come to Kentucky by 1799 and, a generation later, moved across the Ohio River into Indiana. I had no idea that some of my grandmother's ancestors had also come to the same place in Kentucky about the same time.

I had been so startled by Sam's calling the name, Tom Johnson, and his information about Tom's mother being half French, as well as half Cherokee, that I am only now wondering why my father didn't tell me the whole story that summer I was eight, just before my mother moved me to Charlotte with her.

I can still see him as he stood in the doorway of the room where I played on the floor that evening. "Remember, Ella," he said, "you are named for my mother."

"Yes, my grandmother who was Cherokee," I looked up as I answered.

His tall presence leaned slightly against the door frame and his quiet "No" surprised me.

"What were your mother's people if they were not Cherokee?" I asked, for I had understood they were Cherokee, like Lemond.

All these years later, I can see the look on my father's face, his pause, his trying to think what to answer. He spoke after what seemed to me a wait and said, "They were French."

French! I couldn't imagine French, it sounded so fancy. At that time, I had no idea of the extensive contact Cherokees had with the French in the 1600s and earlier 1700s, before the English defeated the

French. I thought my daddy was trying to say something to comfort me, if his mother were not Cherokee, if I were not part Cherokee.

Then I remembered his uncle who had lived in the western Cherokee Nation, who kept up with my daddy by mail after his mother died. "What about your Uncle Tom?" I said. "He was Cherokee."

"Put it out of your mind," my father told me gently, firmly.

So I did, because I trust my father. But it keeps coming back and back and back.

This week, I received a letter with more explanation from Cousin Sam. A French girl raised by Cherokees in the mountains of North Carolina (according to Sam's family story, though it would more likely be the daughter of a Cherokee woman by a French trapper) married a Cherokee man in the 1730s or so. Their French/Cherokee daughter married a man named Alonso, and they were the parents of Tom Johnson (the earlier Tom, born in North Carolina about 1750 to 1755, my grandmother's ancestor, not her brother in the western Cherokee Nation some years later). The earlier Tom was married to a Cherokee and down through the line of their sons, grandsons and great grandsons, Sam was emphatic, Johnson men have married Indian women.

It was in the earlier 1800s that a Johnson was on the land plot next to my father's kin in Elizabethtown, Kentucky, and to the family with Lemond's last name. Towards the end of the 1700s, Sam said, a Johnson had lived more southwest, close to the Mississippi River. I didn't think to ask if that were Tom and his Cherokee wife.

My father would have known much of this from his Uncle Tom, I feel sure. Why wouldn't he tell me his mother was Cherokee? Did he think I was too young to understand? Was he concerned about segregation I might encounter, if I talked about it in the city of Charlotte where I was going to live with my mother?

His silence doesn't tally with the friendship I saw between him and Lemond, the love that showed when he spoke of his mother, his naming me for her, my grandmother I never knew.

But where did the name Alonso come from!

February 9th

In the wee hours of this morning, I had a birthday gift. Luke came upstairs to see me. Asleep, I felt a presence and opened my eyes to find him standing close beside the bed, studying me. He has just started sleeping inside the kitchen and had never before come upstairs. I was surprised and, next to his strong jaws, felt a moment of concern that he might have become rabid. The warning of friends, that wolf/dogs can unexpectedly turn on the person who cares for them, also passed through my head.

Yet, I saw only curiosity in Luke's eyes before he looked away. He had never seen me lying down before, and I reached out my hand to touch the warm fur around his ears. After circling a small oval rug beside the bed three times, Luke settled on it. It took me a while to get used to the sound of his breathing. Then, I slept a contented sleep.

February 15th

One of the pleasures of each day is observing and following tracks in snow and, with Luke on leash, he doesn't disturb these prints before I can look at them. It is interesting to see what Luke's paws look like in snow, different from dog prints with Luke's more in a line, one behind another. I keep hoping to see tracks of the huge buck, the large Vs with the parallel slide marks behind, but haven't.

Seeing raccoon tracks makes me uneasy and I have, after all, started carrying a thick walking stick. I've never liked the idea of a stick but am toting it along, when I don't forget and leave it propped beside the porch door. I remember how safe I felt here last winter before coming face to face with the man who shined the light in my eyes, and before the raccoon's attack. I am thankful for Luke, most of all thankful to know him.

We are almost half way through his quarantine. He is sleeping here by the desk as I write, and I like his close company.

February 19th

Though very cold at times, February has been mild for the most part. The roadbed has, much of the month, been dry and frozen hard enough to drive the Jeep in and out and leave it parked near the house. So I accepted an invitation from my good friends, Ann and Frank, to come to a dinner at their house last night. The evening's invitation included a request that each guest share something creative that they do or have done.

Before the evening was over, Ann sang an Irish song and I like to hear her sing, especially Irish songs. Frank read aloud, a custom I have enjoyed since childhood when my old friends, Elizabeth's family, read aloud to each other with me sometimes included. Will was there at Ann and Frank's and played the Irish whistle, always good music. I picked up a few more tips on playing the one he gave me.

Recently, I've been finding I can play along with tapes I'm familiar with if, and only if, I'm very relaxed, almost in another brain mode. Since I don't drink or smoke, I'm not always that relaxed, but still have a good time, when alone, playing along as best I can with Irish tapes. Luke will sit with me for awhile with his expression of interest, then get up and go out on the sun porch. I'm not sure if that is an indictment of my playing or Luke's acutely sensitive hearing.

For my contribution to the party last night, I read something short that I wrote this winter, a light memory. Other than the description of the old cabin, it is not something strongly felt, as all too much of my writing is. My friends looked surprised when I read it, then laughed.

Mr. Russian

The iron bed was the approximate center of a childhood summer world. A river rushed in front of the cabin and looped upstream into rapids. Down river loomed a bridge and behind the cabin sprang a wild place where bears grew. Half of one bedroom wall was screen wire, no rooms had ceiling, the world slipped in. Once from the drowsy safety of the bed, I attended the excitement of a black bear outside the cabin. Nightly, in soft kerosene light, small mice peered down from rafters in the peaked tin roof, with the curiosity with which I watched them. The river laughed over rocks and gentled me to sleep. Birdsong woke me mornings, if muted steps of fishermen's boots had not.

That morning, Mr. Russian did not get up on time. He should have been up and dressed and out on the river with the others. Always he had been on his fishing visits before, but this morning he was slow. When I climbed my bed's iron head rail and stood in it, because I was used to climbing it, my head stretched over the partition wall and, to my surprise, Mr. Russian stood below.

He had just stepped out of his pajamas, he stood there in pink glory, eyes bulging, too startled to think what to do. I giggled, and he stood there, pear-shaped, pink-skinned and white-haired, not the imposing fly fisherman he was in waders and boots and long-sleeved shirt. That I recall, Mr. Russian was never again one of the fishermen who came back.

March

March 2nd

The daily walks with Luke refresh me and ground me in this place, this future. Yet, I find myself wondering about the human events that have no doubt taken place on this land over the centuries. I have seen only one arrowhead here and am curious about the large collection that Ruth and Elliot have found adjacent to this land, all of which was once Cherokee territory. Now, during these months when Luke is not a passenger in the Jeep, would be a good time for me to stop and ask to see the arrowheads and stone tools again. The University told them that some of the pieces are very, very old, especially the stone tools.

I don't want Luke to have time, while waiting in the Jeep, to scent and get interested in Elliot's livestock, to remember and be enticed across the property line when he is free again. At the moment, he seems to like it fine here by the desk.

March 9th

Despite a real possibility of rabid animals, Luke and I walked last night to my place of beginnings. Our entry to that high meadow was through the cold, wet air from upper spring. As we climbed the rise, the moon was damp and close, and stars seemed near touching. That ridge, where land is friend to talk to and animals answer, is where I learned to stand alone and discovered myself joined to all life. With events of these past two months, I had almost forgotten its luminous feel at night.

I suspect it did Luke good, too, to go up there after dark. The more I get to know him, the more I realize how entirely different he is from dogs that I have been around all my life. How much Luke is like a wolf, I have little way of knowing though I read everything I find about wolves in the library. And Kathy, the vet, is certain that he is in large part gray wolf, as was the veterinarian who treated him when found injured, Carin has told me. It is my sense that Luke is neither wolf nor dog, yet both. Caught between, different than and more than, not a half and half compromise, he is his very own self.

Maybe, I am caught between, too, with grandparents of different cultures. The grandmother I knew, who told me stories, who grew up between the wild North Carolina coast and a dismal swamp, I loved very much. The story of my father's mother, whom I have wished to know, seems to be finding me. My father's very Irish father, whom I remember bedridden in his nineties, sat up in bed to sing Irish songs with gusto. My mother's father was noted in a Norfolk newspaper as that large port's honest police chief during World War I. I've seen the old newspaper, happy to read about this grandfather I barely knew.

March 17th

It's been a fast year since last year's blizzard and almost a year since Luke came. I must be getting old for time to whiz past so fast, yet I don't feel old. Had an enjoyable visit today with a man over the state line, who lives on property with a clearly defined line of acidic soil on one side and alkaline on the other. It was easy to see the different kinds of plant growth in each type of soil. Best of all was spotting raven nests high on a rock cliff, though I didn't see the ravens. I felt the wish to see ravens, here, on this land.

There was a narrow and shallow brook below the cliff, and I jumped lightly from stone to stone above the trickling water, as I listened to the man talk about different types of flora. He walked along the bank and pointed out plants that would start blooming soon. This could be an interesting article, and he invited me to come back. I returned home with a list he has put together of what plants generally indicate which type of soil.

I keep thinking of ravens. Luke appears to be dreaming of something, here on the floor by the desk. I would like to know more of what goes through his keen mind.

March 27th

It's been a busy week preparing gardens. I was getting ready to start early planting until an unexpected and powdery snow yesterday. Ann called and suggested I come over for a moonlit night walk on their farm. The snow was dry and I had left the Jeep on top the ridge rather than all the way out to the state road, so I went. It was a beautiful night, and Ann and I walked until nearly midnight when I drove back and on down the roadbed, the Jeep sliding easily the last stretch of dry snow.

I wished for Luke on the walk and found it hard to leave him behind, here. I think he found it hard, too, and I sat with him a good while when I got back though it was very late. Long past my bedtime and his.

Luke's quarantine will be over soon.

April

April 1st

    Another surprise snow today. Though it didn't stick, it is fun to see Luke frisk in falling snow, even on leash. We spent most of the day out of doors, coming in occasionally for me to warm up with hot tea. Luke watches me with his usual look of interest when I do little things like drink a cup of tea. When I set the tea cup down this afternoon, he was sitting beside me on the floor and reached over with a gentle lick to my hand, not the cup.

April 7th

    Two days ago, I was notified that Luke's quarantine would be over at the end of yesterday. So early this morning, with another light snow falling, I let Luke out into the yard, free. He turned and waited for me to come with him, as I had each morning for three months. I walked into the yard and, still, Luke hesitated as though leashed. So I started up the ridge path with him, a slipover sweater the only extra clothing I had on for warmth. A short way up, Luke evidently got a scent and took off. My heart lifted to see him disappear into tree cover and even more, later, to hear him lightly paw the sun porch door to come in. Despite snow, our winter is over.

April 14th

    A few days after Luke's quarantine ended, it snowed large wet flakes that briefly covered trees and ground, yet now the yard is fragrant with lilac. I have opened house windows for the scent and warm air to come inside. Earlier today, a female cardinal flew to the window over this desk where I sit writing. She continued to return to the window and perch on the sill next to the screen, as though visiting. When I went into the kitchen to fix lunch, this brownish cardinal came to the ledge of the open double windows, repeatedly. I went upstairs to get something, and she hit gently against the screen of the bedroom window. I wondered how she knew I had gone upstairs and felt there was something I should understand, and don't. She was not waiting for bird food, for I don't feed the birds other than to plant bushes with seeds and berries that add to natural supply.

I returned to the kitchen, and the female cardinal again followed to those downstairs windows. From it, I also saw a male in the althea hedge nearby. Was he the red cardinal that struck his feet against the bedroom window just before Luke came last year? I wonder.

Luke has been busy re-exploring the farm and marking territory. Now that his world has expanded again and tick season is underway, I call him to the sun porch to sleep at night rather than upstairs. He appeared surprised by that at first, but has settled back into the porch. Somehow, he appears softer than before the quarantine though no less strong or in good shape, to judge from his sprints across the ridge.

Each of the past three late afternoons, an almost white skunk has followed Luke and me up the meadow ridge and stayed a distance behind. Luke seemed unconcerned. At first, I wondered if the skunk were going to catch up and spray us or, worse, if it might be rabid which worried me. Yet before we got to the high meadow each evening, the unusual looking animal disappeared into woods that run alongside and down to an old pile of handmade brick, which I had in mind to use. Until now, I understand, they are the skunk's home.

April 18th

From the large garden by the river, I can watch Luke run across the bottom land. From there and from gardens around the house, I see him up and down ridges that surround the house, a sight I hope will stay in my heart as long as it beats.

Got onions in the ground and have been thinking about potatoes. I've found a store interested in selling organic potatoes after fall harvest, so will plant more than what I usually plant for myself and people who will venture down the roadbed to buy unsprayed potatoes. Since it is usually young couples who will brave the road, because they want to feed their young child good potatoes, I often give them away. The easy thing about potatoes is the yearly rather than ongoing harvest, other than early ones I dig for summer meals. In the root cellar, they store well for winter, usually a very dependable staple food.

On a walk as the sun set tonight, I noticed the delicacy of color outside, cameo pink over silver sky and dark shapes of trees. It looked peaceful, a peacefulness that I feel as I think of Jena and Sarah doing well with their pregnancies. The babies will come soon.

April 25th

A rainy spell has given me reading time, and I brought back another library book about the Cherokee, last trip into town. From it, I learned something new that caught my attention. Efforts of the Cherokee warrior, Dragging Canoe, and the warriors who fought with him to stop encroachment of white settlers on Cherokee land in western North Carolina and north Georgia, ended by the mid 1790s. Dragging Canoe, who had been in close touch with Tecumseh's resistance in Ohio, was dead. Remaining warriors, some with bounties on their heads, went westward to the Ohio river valley or the French area of Missouri which is surprisingly close to Elizabethtown, Kentucky, where Tom Johnson went at that same time.

A number of these warriors, my reading informs me, were sons of Cherokee mothers and Caucasian fathers who sided with the Cherokee in their struggle to hold on to their mountain land on the North Carolina/Tennessee and north Georgia borders. Along with full blood warriors, the mixed bloods had fought on after the death of Dragging Canoe until they saw that retaliation brought continued hardship to Cherokee women and children, with settlers burning villages, crops and food supplies.

At this time, according to Cousin Sam, the earlier Tom Johnson, who I think would have been the great, great, great, grandfather of my grandmother, left the North Carolina/Tennessee border not far from here. Going by way of Ohio which was Tecumseh's territory, the Shawnee chief who had been in touch with Dragging Canoe's resistance, Tom and his Cherokee wife and at least one son settled just west of Elizabethtown, Kentucky near the Mississippi. That is very close to the French area of Missouri, close to Dragging Canoe's surviving warriors!

Could this ancestor of mine and/or his son have been among those warriors when Dragon Canoe was alive? Is it coincidence that my ancestor, more than once, was in the same time and place as Dragging Canoe or his warriors?

I keep telling myself that surely it is, yet it seems a lot of coincidence. I have admired stories of Dragging Canoe's strong stand against giving up more Cherokee land, his foresight about this loss. I can also appreciate the stand for peace taken by his cousin or sister, Nancy Ward. Nannehi was her Indian name, and she had the status of Beloved Woman of the Cherokees. She also had a daughter married to a European descended settler and grandchildren by him.

Places, dates, people and circumstances keep bumping into each other, and I still know nothing of my paternal grandmother's mother, not even her name. Why is there no family record or remaining memory of her name! Was it an Indian name, hard to remember or spell? I wonder about this silence and remember Sam's insistence that Johnson men, down the line, married Indian women. Who was my grandmother's mother, my great grandmother? It is a strange silence.

Though Luke sleeps on the sun porch now that it's tick season again, he often comes into the downstairs during evening. He's here now, dozing on his side with paws gracefully stretched out before him, eyes closed with ears and nose still alert, I can see. His deep, ridged chest breathes evenly throughout the almost imperceptible movements of his face. Suddenly, as now, he'll open his eyes and look at me watching him and sleepily shut them again.

April 30th

Came in wildly happy tonight at the unity of an endeavor Paul and Jimmy, they who like the fragrance of this house, helped me with today. We mowed the flat meadow by the river, the part not in garden, with an old McCormick #9 horse drawn mower that's been in the barn forever. The wooden shafts of the mower and large rake had trailer hitches on them, so we could pull them behind the Jeep to which I had the same size ball attached. It took some experimenting to pull a mower built for a horse's pace with a car, even a Jeep. We had to gear it down as low as possible and drive very slowly. Paul did a good job behind the wheel, and Jimmy sat the old McCormick #9 well and worked the sickle bar blades. I rode shot gun in the Jeep's passenger seat, with head out the window, despite the Jeep's exhaust fumes, to relay signals from mower to driver. And keep an eye on Jimmy's safety.

For awhile, Luke watched from the shade of the wood's edge, then headed for the ridge and was sitting near the sun porch when I got back to the house late in the afternoon. To use hay as mulch for the garden, I'll gradually rake it with an old wooden hand rake that's also been in the barn forever. My father's curved handle scythe is there, too unwieldy for me to use, too memorable not to keep.

May

May 1st

When I went downstairs to let Luke out this morning, I remembered today is May 1st. On this morning two years ago, I stood before the glass door of the sun porch looking out at the eastward sky, as I held a cup of tea in my hands. All of a sudden, a tiny whirl of color crashed into a pane of glass, just on the other side of the middle of my forehead, startling me so much that I spilled tea. Lying on the step on the other side of the door was a ruby throated hummingbird. I opened the door, saw the bird was dead and picked it up, sad at its stillness. As I looked at the shimmering green and rose in my hand, something tangible shot through me and I somehow knew that my mother was dying.

Though I had returned from her home just the afternoon before, I ran into the house to call her. I had spent two weeks with her, for she had been sick, and came home because she was better. I had thought to get potatoes in the ground and then go back and stay another week or more with her.

The woman who had cared for my mother for several years answered the phone and immediately said, "I was just getting ready to call you. I think you had better come."

I rushed to throw on clothes, grab my still unpacked bag and retrace the drive I had made just the day before. I sang and said prayers for my mother all during the long drive to Charlotte and hoped I would get there in time for her to know, for me to tell her again that I love her. Though we were very different from each other.

I did get there in time for her to know and had been sitting beside her bed for some hours, when the rhythmic rasp of her breathing stopped. It took me a few minutes, maybe only seconds, to understand the sudden quietness. For a ring of light had surrounded her bed and surprised me. Even though I had said aloud only a few minutes before, "Mama, it's all right to go. You won't be alone."

Several weeks after she died, I dreamed of her one early morning. She wore a bright orange dress and looked very happy. I felt close to her and knew—the lack of understanding that can distance people in life is not necessarily there after death. This morning, as I remembered my mother, I let Luke out and he turned and looked at me a long moment. He trotted across the road and beyond a bush, then to the stream that flows from the springs. He looked back again before he took off up the ridge.

I stood at the door and watched, as he disappeared into rhododendron, and thought of the grand baby due this week, my mother and father's first great grandchild, my grand child—the circle that is life.

May 4th

Jena's baby arrived today, a boy, and all are fine. I will go in a few days to meet my first grandchild and drop Luke at Carin's. She said she could take care of him there, at least for a couple of days, and would like to see him. She's too busy with her own farming to come here.

I've always known that grandchildren would be important to me. For my granny, my maternal grandmother that I knew, mattered to me very much. She understood what I said or didn't say, I loved her and liked to listen to her stories. And to her prayers that she said on her knees after she thought me asleep, when I slept with her on yearly visits. Learning about my other grandmother, who died when my father was young, matters to me, deeply.

Being a grandmother sneaked up on me. So recently, it seems, I held my children in my arms, watched them grow and discover themselves. Now they will do the same, as life completes itself. A new adventure for them, a new one for me, and a big adventure ahead for the babies.

May 12th

My first grandson fit into my arms just right. I have happy pictures in my head of him and his happy mama and daddy, but the most vivid memory of the overnight with them is the feel of young Clay in my arms.

I had wondered if I would wish that I were the one nursing this baby, for nursing my babies was one of the happiest things of my life. However, the Creator, it seems, planned it well. I was quite content to rock this baby, watch him sleep, sing and dance with him in my arms when he was wakeful, and at bedtime hand my grand baby to his loving mama and go myself to sleep. Luke did well at Carin's.

May 18th

Today, I did something that disturbs me deeply. Luke returned from a run with a squirrel latched onto his chest, just under his throat where he could not get to it. He sat outside the sun porch, very quiet and looking perplexed, with this animal under his nose, the squirrel clutching Luke's fur for all it was worth. Immediately, I wondered if the squirrel were rabid, since it's behavior seemed strange. And I know that any squirrel will bite so, even with thick gloves, I did not try to pull it off. With Luke still, and he was surprisingly still, I hoped that the squirrel would relax its grip on him and jump to freedom. It didn't and, eventually, I felt that I had to do something because of the possibility of rabies.

Wearing heavy work gloves, I positioned long handled lopper blades around the squirrel's throat. I hoped to cut off the squirrel's head so quickly that it would not suffer. Agonizing about this, I did not think to sharpen the blades, and now agonize about that. For the cut was not fast and clean, and it tore me to see this little animal cringe as I whacked. It was awful! But once started, I had to finish as quickly as possible.

Luke sat quietly with this going on and appeared relieved at my efforts to help. With the second try, the squirrel's head fell off and, with gloves still on, I pulled the small body off of Luke's chest. Then, I saw the underneath side of the squirrel, its full tits, and knew her to be a nursing mother that had tried a desperate trick to save her babies. Or herself, so that she could get back to feed them.

Now at bedtime, I am sitting here at the desk with thoughts of her babies, somewhere, waiting for nourishment that will not come, of the alarm the mother must have felt and her efforts to get back to her young. At sunset, I sat in the porch swing for a long time, just letting myself be, and thought of the valiant squirrel that I killed out of my fear. I hope I will always remember her.

Luke sat nearby with his eyes averted, as though watching the sunset. Was this inherent courtesy on his part or what? I noticed it because in recent months, he has not turned his gaze away so quickly as he used to. I have tried to be more thoughtful in my looking too directly or long at him. And have remembered that, as a child, I knew not to look right at anything or anyone. It wasn't seemly. Later, in the outside workaday world, I was told that I must look people in the eye and learned to do that though, now, I question its courtesy. Unless with someone or something you feel very close to.

Am glad there will be moonlight coming through the bedside windows tonight, for I don't know how much I will sleep, thinking of the squirrel babies. It reminds me to be even more thankful for the blessing of Jena's healthy child, and that Sarah is doing well as her time nears. I keep remembering my grandson's sweet, round face and the feel of him in my arms.

May 25th

     Everything is planted except corn, which I'll start next week. Had my first swim of the season earlier this week. The river was cold and cold and felt exuberantly good to me, once I got a little used to it. Am catching up on writing and editing, now that most of the garden is in. My glimpses of Luke, here and there on the farm, remind me of him this time last year. I feel the bond between us now.

June

June 4th

A momentary gardening lull gives space to bring together more information from Sam about my father's ancestors, the fragmented stories from my own family, available census records and other historical information. This combination of the documented and undocumented, put in chronological order, takes on shape, light and shadow, surprises. Such as an obvious reason my grandmother grew up in Kansas!

That her mother and the four children up and went to Kansas after the father went off to fight for the Union in 1861 was the story I heard most in my family. It always bothered me, for why would they do that? How could the father find them when he returned from the war between the states?

The southeastern corner of Kansas, where my grandmother and her mother ended up and where Lemond's paternal grandmother and grandfather later came, was known as Neutral Territory at the time of the Civil War, if I understand correctly. It bordered western Indian Territory and the Cherokee area where my grandmother had been born. She turned two soon after the war began.

Not only did her father fight for the Union, which is well known, I now read that many or most western Cherokee men fought for the Union. Particularly the very traditional faction, called Pins because they designated themselves by wearing crossed pins on their shirts. I don't know any way to find out if my great grandfather was a Pin, a traditionalist. Like his ancestor, Tom Johnson, who left the eastern Cherokee area and went west the same time and place as Dragging Canoe's warriors, my grandmother's father and his family were in certain places, at particular times, where unusual events took place. It could be coincidence, or not.

When men left for the war, women and children and old people were left unprotected from outlaws that flocked into the unprotected Indian Territory and from other factions that wrecked havoc there. I am reading that several thousand, some sources say ten thousand, people from tribes in western Indian Territory fled thievery, starvation and worse to take refuge in the southeastern part of Kansas that offered some Federal protection though little food, I've read. History now calls these thousands "war refugees," though I never heard about them in school. Was my grandmother a child refugee, like countless children in war torn countries today? She, her brothers and sister and mother went to the very place, at the same time, as these thousands of American Indian refugees. Could such hardships account for the health problems of my grandmother's life and her younger sister's even younger death?

Their father survived the war, our family story goes, and was killed by bushwhackers along the Cimarron River on his way home, which always seemed sad to me. His companions evidently knew, or learned, the whereabouts of his family and brought word of his death. My grandmother would have been, by then, close to six years old and stayed in southeastern Kansas with her widowed mother. Because the structure of life had been destroyed in Indian Territory, as well as southwestern Missouri, it would have been very hard for a widow to return.

It was Ella's older brother, Tom Johnson, who eventually settled in the western Cherokee Nation, married a Cherokee woman and later, after his sister's death, maintained ongoing correspondence with her youngest son, my father. This brother's name, Tom Johnson, and names of the other brother, George, who went to the gold fields of California, of my grandmother, Ella, and also her sister, Belle, are all on late 1800s rolls. Though the ages listed are of a generation later than my grandmother and her siblings. Very likely these names were descendants of my father's Uncle Tom, his mother's brother. His children or grandchildren bearing family names.

Was Tom on an earlier roll? Or was he was one of the many

traditional Cherokee who, I am reading, refused, absolutely refused as a matter of principle, to register for a federal roll? Or did he go by a Cherokee name? Many things, I do not know.

After they married about 1885, my grandmother and grandfather, the Irish one who came to Kansas from Indiana and whose grandmother had been raised among the Potowami and Miami Indians, lived in a sod house in the grass lands of Kansas before returning east. In blizzard weather, they brought the cow into their sod home, my favorite of my family's stories.

Have also learned that, among the matrilineal Cherokee, where children were of the mother's family and clan, fathers were not excluded. Yet, it was maternal uncles who were responsible for a sister and her children. My father's Uncle Tom, my grandmother's brother, must have been aware of this responsibility, for it was he who kept up ongoing correspondence with my father after his mother died when he was about twelve.

It occurs to me, as I sit here writing, that Lemond's grandfather, Levi, who as a very young man stayed in the Linville Gorge during the 1838 federal removal of Cherokees to the west, yet who with his wife left North Carolina for Kansas by the 1870s, the same area of Kansas where my grandmother was growing up, may have gone there to carry out a Cherokee responsibility to a younger sister, or sister's daughter, and her children who were refugees of war.

That my grandmother's mother, whose name I have not known, may have been a niece or younger sister of Lemond's grandfather or perhaps of his wife, Caroline Paine, who ended up on the official western Cherokee roll after Levi's death. That the friendship between the families of my father and of Lemond may go back a long way!

Such coincidence that parallels history, though not proof, gives heat to cold stories, vivid color and form to skimpy information strained down through scattered families and time. And possible, though startling, light to long shadowed space, a shadow I have felt and am trying to understand.

June 12th

Luke and I were walking up the ridge toward the high
meadow today when I noticed two birds high overhead, flying
towards south. They looked black in color and, watching their
flight, I thought them ravens. Back at the house, I checked the
bird book and, sure enough, the wing span and tail shape looked
from the ground like the underside drawing of a common raven in
the bird book. I've heard that, just as there is somehow a working
symbiosis between hawk and deer, ravens have maintained a hunting
relationship with wolves.

I pondered the meaning of the direction, south, the direction
they flew, and think it is connected with the concept of summer, the
fullness of a cycle. Perhaps that is where Luke and I are in our lives,
both individually and in our life together, in the fullness of it, like the
two ravens flying south.

June 17th

Another grandson, born today! Another healthy baby, and
Sarah is doing well though, unexpectedly, had a cesarean. She asked
if I could come help out when she goes home from the hospital
tomorrow and said it would be fine to bring Luke, that he could
stay in the house. So we will leave here in the morning. Little Vic
is brown haired, I'm told, as was his mama when she was born. His
young cousin, only a few weeks older, is blond like his mama. Our
family is blessed and blessed.

June 27th

It was a wonderful week with Sarah and her family, though,
mostly, she took care of Vic upstairs, as he nursed and slept. I
cooked and kept things going downstairs and had happy times of

rocking Vic when he was awake, and noticing the deep look in his eyes. All my life that I can remember, I have liked to hold animals, dolls, babies. But the very best part of being a grandmother is the pleasure of beginning to know these two boys who are my grandsons!

Luke seemed to enjoy our visit, too. He claimed a large carpeted stair near the bottom of the staircase for his place, where a turn in the stairs made a cave like effect. It was interesting to me to see how repeatedly he chose that spot. Carpet on the stairs and a nearby ceiling fan must have added comfort, yet I sensed that it was the right angle of the staircase walls that drew Luke to that protected corner. He could see what was coming from any direction.

Sarah's golden retriever/lab, a female, was more than tolerant of Luke and, though the cat hissed and spat at him, Luke casually ignored the cat. Maybe that's why she hissed and spat.

I stopped on the way home for a night at Jena's to visit Clay again. Getting to hold both babies, in turn, each so special, was quite a week.

June 30th

The black mulberry tree I planted a few years ago is bearing for the first time, and I have been climbing in it to eat my fill of berries, juice running down my arms and chin, and staining my clothes. Have even tracked purple footprints onto the kitchen floor with bare feet.

As I scrubbed the floor, thinking about bills due, things that need to be fixed, and my purple stained clothing, I laughed at the thought that to stand naked when under a mulberry tree would make a lot of sense. Like living with the courage of an open heart.

That Luke likes berries, I had not imagined until I dropped some. He picked each one up, skillfully, with his small front teeth and ate them with what looked like much pleasure. From then on, I matched berry for berry, one for him for every one I ate. Perched on the low tree limb, I placed each one of his onto his agile tongue as I ate mine with other hand.

Though most of the mulberries were too high on the tree for Luke to reach, this afternoon I saw him use those precise front teeth to pluck each of the first ripe blueberries from their lower bush near the mulberry tree. I suppose that wolves in the wild do eat wild berries. Probably plain dogs do, too, if they have opportunity.

July

July 7th

Years ago, my father's only sister, younger than he, asked me to search, someday, for the grave of their mother's father along the long Cimarron. Receiving news of her husband's death by bushwhackers on the banks of this river, my great grandmother sent money by the messenger for a stone marker, says our family story. The Cimarron runs through parts of Oklahoma, Kansas, perhaps neighboring states, and information of the grave's location has not survived, if the marker has. Yet, it stays with me that I told Aunt Madge, who as a young child may have said the same to her mother before she died, I will try to find it someday. Someday.

On that same visit to my aunt, soon after my own father's death, she described her mother, my grandmother. Both she and an older aunt by marriage, one who as a very young bride had taken care of my dying grandmother, pointed to my cheekbones and called them "exactly" like my grandmother's. They were emphatic, I have her bone structure though my grandmother had straight, cold black hair and "olive" skin, they called it. I don't have black hair, but do have olive skin, so dermatologist say.

I wondered why Aunt Madge added "with no fuzz of Celtic hair on it," for I didn't know, then, that lack of facial hair can be an indication of American Indian blood. Now, I understand that she wanted to talk with me of our Indian heritage and hesitated, not sure if I knew, if my mother wanted me to know. Or if my father wanted me to know.

I wasn't sure what I knew either, for he had told me his mother's people were French. At the time of visiting my aunt, my thoughts were on the loss I felt that he was suddenly gone from my life, just when I had reached the place that I could go on my own to see him.

Aunt Madge also spoke of the old pair of Indian moccasins my grandmother had brought east from Kansas. After she and my grandfather moved to north Georgia, my father, youngest of their five sons, was born there not far below the North Carolina line. The area had been prime Cherokee land before the Removal, more than fifty years before. Now, I realize that my grandmother's maternal grandparents, whose names I do not know, were most likely forced from that very place in 1838 and were on the Trail of Tears, it is called. That the old moccasins my grandmother brought east most likely returned to the place from which they had walked!

They were later lost in a fire that destroyed my grandparents' home and everything in it, Aunt Madge told me. Then Ella, my grandmother, died though not from the fire. Any information of her parents must have gone up in flames along with the moccasins. For the Bible that my grandfather had in later life, the information available now, held birth and death dates only of his family, not my grandmother's. Her birth/death dates are in there, and I know from family stories that my grandfather loved and missed her the rest of his life. From Cousin Sam and my father, I know about his Uncle Tom, my grandmother's brother, yet nothing of my grandmother's mother. I believe there is a connection between her and Lemond's family. Perhaps, something in me some how knew and that is why Lemond meant so very much to me.

July 20th

Last night, I thought Luke was going to go through the sun porch wall. I heard him from my bedroom above the sun porch and kitchen, the sound of his strong body hitting against the wall, repeatedly. And a deep sound of anxiety, or angst, that came from inside of him. Growling, I suppose it was, deep and intense, for he didn't bark. I looked out the bedroom window, down on the dark yard, and could see nothing so went cautiously downstairs. Instead of letting Luke outside, as he wanted, I brought him from the sun porch into the kitchen with me. For I didn't know what might be out in the night, a gun or lethal claws or teeth. I didn't think whatever it was would brave Luke to try to come inside.

When he continued to heave himself against the kitchen wall, I called the sheriff's office and a deputy came. After a reasonable time, his marked car drove slowly down the very rutted and, therefore, noisy road. When from a window, I saw the uniform and hat emerge from the car and nothing happened, I went outside to talk with him. I still didn't let Luke out, for I figured he would take off after whatever had been there.

"It must have been a bear," the deputy said. "Black bears do cross this area and that would explain your dog's actions." He had looked for car tracks or foot prints on the roadbed and hadn't noticed any.

Bear was probably right. What he didn't see, and I didn't until this morning, was a fresh looking cigarette butt in the yard, several feet from the sun porch. I doubt it was put there by Smoky Bear, yet wolves are said not to be good watch dogs in regard to people. The electric meter box is near that part of the yard; maybe the man who reads it had earlier stomped out a cigarette.

July 27th

Chicory blooms a purplish blue along gravel roads into town, each flower head holding memories of summers of chicory along unpaved mountain roads. As wild flower colors became deeper purple, I would know another growing up summer, my treasured time in the mountains, was winding down, the return to Charlotte near. When the Joe Pye bloomed rich and full, it was almost time to go. Am happy that, now, I can stay.

There has been no more jumping up on walls or growling or whatever it was from Luke. Quiet summer nights and brief rains. I am spending time in the river, Luke has dug his shady hollows under shady bushes. We visit in the cool of evening, each of us sitting on the planks of the sun porch floor, as small breezes come from one wall of windows through the other.

July 31st

Jena called and asked if I could come help with Clay for several weeks. His daddy, who has been doing an excellent job of taking care of him so Jena could go back to her job, fell and broke his right arm. Carin will take Luke, since it worked out well when I left him there recently. He and I will be off in the morning. Fortunately, the onions are in and drying in the barn. Potatoes can wait until fall to be harvested. The house painter, scheduled for this coming week, said that he would go ahead and paint the outside of the house as planned, since he doesn't have to come in. It will be the same cream color that is almost green, green that is almost cream.

Fragrant shrubs and bushes with berries, local wild flowers of various shapes and colors, the terraced herb and kitchen garden, some evergreens and other young trees are beginning to encircle the house with a journey of seasons. The large garden in the bottom by the river is terraced raised beds, potatoes inter-planted with the small lavender flowers of flax to deter bugs. A friend, who saw it recently, stood in surprise and commented that it was the most feminine farm he had ever seen. It is a pretty sight.

Naturally curving lines please my eye and make sense with the contour of the land though I also appreciate, very much appreciate, lines. For a circle is too enclosed until opened by a line, and a line doesn't rest until part of a circle. That eternal and wonderful enigma of yin and yang, the feminine and the masculine, we women and men!

Still 1994

Earlier this month Luke and I arrived back at the farm, and the house looked fresh and pretty in the afternoon light, with its new coat of cream green paint. I let Luke out of the Jeep, and he trotted to the bushes across the roadbed from the house and then to the branch that comes from the springs. After I carried an armful of things into the house and opened windows, we walked down to the river. I sat on its bank to listen to the rush of water over rock, happy to be home though the two months with one of my grand babies and family and new friends had been fun for me, and I think for Luke.

He sniffed the long length of the bottom land and, instead of venturing further, came back and sat with me beside the river. Two mallards floated by on a quiet current of the far side, adding their green and purple to the sun glinted water. Luke watched with intent interest, a quiver in his shoulder muscles though he sat quietly. He had been part of a daily small pack of young people who worked on Carin's farm for room and board or produce during the growing season. From what she tells me, they enjoyed Luke and he, them; a new phase in his life.

Within a few days of returning here, I realized he was waiting for food, yet did not ask for it as dogs usually do. He has not seemed to hunt, at least he has brought no kills home for me to see since we got back. So I've been buying dog food for him and fresh chicken thighs for both of us. I cook mine and leave Luke's raw, a meal I see he likes. Other changes came more gradually.

The first priority of the farm, before I started digging the potatoes and marketing them, was to harvest a ripe patch of millet. I had planted it to see how it would grow, and it did well in this somewhat dry summer. Seed of the variety can be threshed from the hull by hand, seed not easily come by, and I wanted to save seed to grow more, for I like to eat millet.

I used a small hand sickle to cut the not too high stalks and grasped a handful in my left hand, as I cut with the small crescent shaped tool in my right. It was easy to bind each bunch with one of its pliable stalks and stack the bunches upright to dry. As I worked, Luke continued to explore the farm and re-mark boundaries, his work, I am beginning to understand and appreciate. I kept an eye out for him and glimpsed him ever so often on the more open spots of one ridge or another. I've learned to make a certain call that seems to carry and he will usually respond by appearing, sometime after, wherever I am. Though it may be a different place from where I was, when I gave the call.

In mid-afternoon of the day I gathered millet, an unexpected job found me, for I wasn't looking for it. The day was surprisingly hot, and I had come back to the house to get water and cool off before going back to the bottom land. As I reached the sun porch, the phone rang from this small front room where I write, and I answered it without stopping in the kitchen for water.

A man on the other end introduced himself as working with the non-profit group that had participated in a meeting I attended in September, at a town near Jena's. The meeting was about the importance of local agriculture, something I believe and am interested in. Afterwards, I had opportunity to talk with the speaker and, as our conversation ended, he said to me, "Promise you will do whatever you are asked to do."

Never imagining that much would be asked, I nodded.

Now, from that same organization, was a phone call asking for my credentials in agriculture. I don't have any, I told the man on the other end, for I have no degree in agriculture.

Growing food just interests me and has, as far back as I can remember. I didn't say that, but what I did tell the man, as excuse for not having much to say, was that I had been harvesting millet all day by hand and was so tired and thirsty I could hardly think what my name was.

He already knew that I had worked as a registered lobbyist on sustainable agriculture issues. However, the fact that I was actually out in a field working was probably what made an impression. For I didn't think to tell this caller that in the latter '80s and early '90s, I had been in the right place at the right time to be in on the beginnings of the Sustainable Agriculture Working Group in North Carolina and then Virginia. Or that I had been asked to testify not only at state legislative committee hearings, but at a governor's environmental hearing and then a U.S. House Agriculture Committee hearing. I wouldn't have told him that my testimony at the latter two created a surprising stir, helpful stirs, at least for the moment.

I hung up the phone, relieved that this caller would surely not recommend me for anything and I could go back to my farming, full time.

A few days ago I was amazed to receive a letter, saying that I had been appointed, yes appointed, to reorganize an agriculture seminar for this well known North American organization in the U.S. and Canada. And put together a meeting in Montreal summer after next and, before that, attend an international meeting in Switzerland this coming summer. I thought I must be reading the letter wrong and called the organization's number in Canada to say I wasn't qualified for the job.

The person who answered, and turned out to be the executive secretary of the organization, assured me that I wasn't reading the letter wrong and could do most of the organizing by mail and phone, with travel away from the farm only a few times a year. As she talked, the thought shot through my head that, all over the world, people get up each day and do jobs they aren't qualified to do, because they need to be done. And I like to learn new things, so I said, yes, I would do my best.

October 29th

A puzzling development here on the farm is that, increasingly, I have found cigarette butts on the road facing the house, though not again in the grass close to the sun porch, as in July before Luke and I left for Jena's. With this unknown and the lingering reports of rabid wildlife, I hesitate to walk in over the ridge at night even with Luke, and I miss that.

Instead, I've made the old roadbed passable most of the time by having it scraped, banked, and graveled, a mundane and now practical entry to my newly painted home. The potatoes I am selling help with that expense, though I won't be growing for market next year. Am already busy with the new job.

Luke is back to sleeping beside my bed, a presence I appreciate though he wakes me at first light each morning. He nudges me gently awake with his moist nose on my forehead, and I get up and go downstairs with him and open the sun porch door. He spends his days out of doors and is an easy companion, who busies himself with his work while I am busy too. We do start out walking together each morning and evening, and Luke still goes off on his own adventures during our walks. Returning, when I am half way or more down the ridge, he reappears and runs down the ridge behind me, gathering speed as he passes.

I call out, "Good job, Luke." And see his pleasure in my pleasure when I arrive back at the sun porch behind him.

We still visit on the floor each evening, though not on the sun porch floor since he comes into the house with tick season over.

December 12th

Winter is when deciduous trees in woods are most beautiful, like old faces that show craft of bone and paths of a lifetime. Luke and I walk the woods a lot to see what we can see, Luke to scent. At least we start out and end up together, though I think he plays a game with me. I go up on the high ridge before the end of our walks, and he finds me and times his return down, exactly, to start after I am part way down. He gathers speed as he passes me and gets to the sun porch door ahead of me. He practically dances with my laughter, my joy in him, as I reach the house several minutes later.

This joy of mine in his ability to run, in him, and my getting up early to let him outside where life is breaking each morning, are what Luke seems to ask of me. He gives much more.

Cousin Sam and his wife came by on their return from a mountain trip and have invited me to visit them in Kentucky, which I hope to do. Sam's letters and this visit have clarified some of the things he told me in Kentucky, when Rob and I spent the intense evening listening to his knowledge of family. I puzzle over the connections between the three families that lived near each other in the early 1800s, as recorded in old Kentucky plot maps. Three families with the surnames of my paternal grandmother, my paternal grandfather, and of Lemond! This information still startles me. And delights me.

I saw young Vic over Thanksgiving and will see Clay during Christmas; each grand son several months old, each very huggable and rivetingly interesting. I am one of their many ancestors!

1995

January 6th

It was a year ago today that the rabid raccoon attacked Luke, a fast year. Since the colder weather began, I have not seen any more cigarette butts on the road across from the house and hope that is the end of it. Have found someone to stay with Luke on the occasions I am gone for this new job, a find that shows promise for Luke's happiness and my new activities. Randy is young enough to want to hike vigorously with Luke and has legs tall enough to come near keeping up with him. Mine are no where near long enough, though I'm not short. Randy is old enough to be responsible, works near enough to this place and is free enough to stay here when I am gone. He says he would like opportunities to be out of doors and on this mountain.

His first stay with Luke will be in two weeks, when I attend a small meeting in Ohio for the agriculture seminar that I am working with. I'll drive to Columbus for the weekend meeting and return through Indiana and Kentucky to do more family research and visit Cousin Sam and Pauline.

Not much snow, so far this winter. I miss seeing Luke in snow.

January, 29th

In a small archives of the Indiana county where a paternal great, great grandfather of mine lived in the early 1800s, I happened on an old newspaper article. It turned out to be about the woman this two greats grandfather married—my great, great grandmother.

Though I had known her name from my grandfather's Bible and something of her paternal grandfather, another ancestor who left Ireland for America in the mid 1700s, I had not known that she was raised among the Potowami or Miami Indians of Clay County! Her father and his brother and their wives, according to the copy of the old paper, chose to live and raise their children among the American Indians there.

Apparently, these Irish Americans were not missionaries or traders or intermarried with native people. It was simply the way they wanted to live, according to the old newspaper. Not surprising with the probable tribal background of their ancestors in the northern part of Ireland or the Hebrides, before the Jacobite defeat in the highlands of Scotland and in Ireland.

This great, great grandmother's family spoke the Indian's language and the children played with the Indian children, the article said. Commenting on how unusual this was in that time and place, the newspaper gave names, dates and other information that tally exactly with the information I had. There is no question that one of these Irish daughters, Ann Christy who came of age in a Potowami/ Miami community, was the grandmother of my paternal grandfather, the Irish one who married my Cherokee grandmother.

This sheds new light, both on him and on my grandmother. Something in me has wanted to know my grandmothers of the past. It feels as though they are making themselves known to me, which wouldn't be a surprising thing for grandmothers to do.

Here at my feet, Luke shows those movements of sleep that may come from dreams. I would like to know what he dreams. And who and what were his fore bearers, especially the wolf one.

August 4th

It was a busy spring and this much of summer, though it whizzed by quietly. Am getting ready to leave for Europe, my first big trip for this new job, a week long, sustainable agricultural meeting in Switzerland and two weeks longer, traveling on my own.

Luke is doing well, and he has had some short stays with Randy here while I made grand children visits. He and Luke do well together, so I am looking forward to this three week adventure overseas.

August 28, 1995
on the plane home

Mentors of much experience appeared at the conference. People I am learning from, places where I spent time, what I am learning are all weaving new threads into me, I can feel. Yet every place, every person, everything circles my heart back to the soft mountains of home with their purples and greens, blues and orange and rose. Back to my family and to Luke.

The trip was fun though and, after the meeting in Switzerland, I took time on my own to revisit places of my ancestors in Ireland and the Hebrides Islands just northeast of Ireland, between Ireland and the northwest coast of Scotland. Places I have been once before.

Before that, en route to the week long meeting in Switzerland, I changed planes in London and spent two nights with Sheila who lives not far from Gatwick Airport. We had a wonderful day hiking on public paths through English farms, stopping frequently at pubs for tea and oat cakes. As Sheila put it, we ate our way across Surrey County.

After the meeting, flying back to the British Isles from Switzerland and flying fairly low, I watched farm rows change from the precise straight lines of Switzerland to more gentle ones as we flew over France. After we crossed the English Channel and I boarded an even smaller plane, we approached Scotland's west coast with farms below noticeably more wild and curving. Then, we flew over a bit of North Sea to the outer chain of islands in the Hebrides. There, potato beds are started by turning sod back over rock that has little soil, laying the seed potatoes on and mulching them with seaweed, thickly. In following years, the seaweed breaks down into soil, where vegetables such as kale can grow. I found these shifting shapes of farming an interesting commentary on the people, as well as topography of each country.

A bus ride from the most northern island of the Outer Hebrides down through the second Isle of Harris to its southern tip, will stay with me as long as I have memory. We rode down the west coast of Harris at sunset, and the ocean caught fire and color washed up the treeless mountains that rise from the sea. We were on a narrow road that wound between mountain and ocean, in the sun's fire, in eternity it felt.

As we came down the mountain and began to pass houses before reaching a darkened small town, the bus driver stopped at several homes to deliver parcels of groceries. Arriving at the bed and breakfast where I spent the night, hot embers of a peat fire waited in the hearth.

Early next morning from Harris and in the company of a priest and several shepherds and their dogs, I caught what looked like a fishing boat that makes a morning run to the small island of Berneray. The men spoke Gaelic, which has the sound of sea that sprayed over us and lapped against huge rocks that rose from the water like whales.

One of the shepherds pointed out golden eagles that circled high in blue sky over turquoise water, as sunshine turned the sea rocks to gold with occasional dark forms of seals upon them. Between waves that rocked the sturdy, open wooden boat and dampened our faces, I watched the sky and listened to the Gaelic that sounded unaccountably familiar to my ears, as the sea felt to my feet.

Later, on a small car ferry from Berneray to North Uist, I talked with the local doctor, also a passenger. He offered me a ride and sight seeing tour as he made house calls on the island of North Uist where he lives, and even took me home to lunch with his wife. From the lower island, South Uist, I caught an all night ferry back to the west coast of Scotland and, for the entire seven hour ride, stood on deck, watching a full, full moon over water, enjoying the feel of sea beneath my feet.

The following day, I took a modern, enclosed and less enjoyable ferry from Scotland to Northern Ireland which, under recent cease fire agreement, was noticeably more relaxed than on my first trip to Belfast several years ago. Then, I had arrived in the Belfast train station and gotten off a train to British soldiers with guns at ready. And a huge gaping hole in the station roof, which had been blown off by a bomb a few days before.

Then, as on this recent trip to Northern Ireland, I walked streets around Belfast where bombs exploded for too many years and soldiers patrolled and stopped and searched those who wore backpacks, as I do. Though my ancestral sympathies are with the native Irish Catholics overtaken by the English, I found British soldiers very courteous. There were still a few of them at checkpoints on this recent trip.

On that earlier trip, right after I had left Belfast, a bomb went off on the very street where I had walked back and forth to the Belfast Library. It hit a car with a family in it, I read in a next day's newspaper.

On this recent and peaceful trip to the north coast of Ireland, I stood at the harbor in Derry where my father's Irish ancestors began their removal, in some ways not different from the Cherokee's. They came to the British colonies of America after the mid 1700s defeat of Jacobite supporters of the Stewart line of kings.

With the wind in my face and the sea before me, I wondered what my fore bearers felt to leave their homeland forever, as the Cherokee and other tribes in the United States were forced to leave theirs, less than a hundred years later. Westward, from the coastlines of Co. Donegal, I gazed west and north, at a white capped and endless Atlantic.

The trip had begun with the meeting in Switzerland, at a lodge on a lake large enough to look like the sea. When I first arrived in Switzerland, I was naively surprised to find no help in English for transportation signs or train announcements. After going into a, fortunately, empty rest room marked "herr" and discovering that it contained men's urinals, I did better and found my way to the ladies room and then to Lake Constance.

It was there, the first evening, that I met two older men who, each, in an unassuming way seems to have taken it upon himself to give me help with this new job. Help I appreciate, for both are men of depth and integrity, intuition and creativity. One has much, much experience in true grass roots community development, and the other knows how to bring such information to others. One is Egyptian, the other American, and the work of each seems to complement that of the other. The Egyptian and his wife will stay over a night here at the farm in December, after a continental meeting that the American has invited me to attend.

During a social hour concluding that first evening in Switzerland, I had been introduced, as a person involved in agriculture, to this tall and regal American and his wife. He acknowledged our introduction with a remark on the importance of agriculture and need for scientific knowledge in third world farming.

I answered, too quickly, that I thought agriculturalist in our, so called, first world could learn from indigenous farmers in every part of the world.

He drew himself up even taller, looked hard at me for a moment before he replied, thoughtfully, "You're right. The problem is they don't know what they know."

His remark hit like an arrow in the middle of my forehead. I keep pondering it and think I am beginning to understand that part of our recognizing and valuing what we know comes by its reflection, in some way, back to us. In the case of colonial arrogance, the reflection back to native people may have been for a long time either negative or confusing.

One of the presenters, whom I especially listened to, was a Polynesian man who spoke with such obvious respect for the village people he had worked with in his extensive experience. On the last full day of the week, after another scheduled speaker could not arrive, I was asked to talk briefly about a comment I had made in group discussion earlier in the week. It was on the subject of what has happened in North Carolina and Virginia counties since the numerous small and locally owned farms have been edged out by a few large farms, often corporately owned or financed and controlled elsewhere.

From lobbying, I still had in my head statistics to back up what I described. With the smaller farms, there were locally grown foods and the small industries connected to them, local tax money for schools, local employment in stores that serviced the many farms and had provided other services to a thriving community, most of which even had a movie theater! Money generated in the community stayed in it, for the most part. With large or corporate farms, there are few of these benefits and most of the money goes out of the county. Even the old movie theaters have closed down, as businesses and towns ceased to thrive.

As I finished this short talk and returned to my seat, the man whose presentations had been of such interest to me caught my eye across the room and gave a thumbs up. He turned to say something to the man next to him and later repeated it to me. He told me that my talk was the most interesting thing that he'd heard all week because it was so real. His was a thoughtful reflection back to me, one that surprised and encouraged me.

The next morning, the week ended with a fun and funny train ride with another interesting and older man from the Pacific. He was leaving on an earlier train to the Geneva Airport than I needed to take for my later flight, but he had made that ride before. Since I was unsure that I would know the airport train stop from loud speaker announcements and signs in a language I didn't understand, I rode the earlier train with him. I knew the airport stop was a small one before Geneva, a stop which this traveling companion said he would recognize. In due time he looked out the window at an approaching station and said, "This is it, let's go."

I picked up my backpack and followed him off the train. Outside, I looked around and knew it wasn't the same station where I had boarded the train a week before. "This is not it," I said.

Surprised, he asked, "Are you sure?"

"Yes," I answered, just as the train started slowly to move.

Without further question, he stepped along with it and reached up one hand to grab the rail of the slowly moving train and pull himself up to the doorstep and held out an arm to help me. I ran alongside as the train started to speed up and hopped on the steps of the still opened train door, back pack in one hand. The next stop was ours, and I felt a new confidence in finding my way.

And too much confidence in hopping onto moving trains. For, early yesterday morning, the overnight train I rode back from Scotland's west coast arrived late in London. Trying to make my flight out of Gatwick, I caught a Black cab to the other downtown train station to catch the airport commuter. It was on the tracks as I came down an escalator, as quickly as possible in the crowd. Just as I reached the train to Gatwick, it started to pull out with a door still open and I reached up to grab the rail and hop on. A uniformed arm pulled me back and said, emphatically, "Madame, that is dangerous."

In frustration, I turned on him and said, "You've just made me miss my plane to the states!"

"Calm down now, calm down," the officer said. "There will be another train in ten minutes."

I waited for it, hoping the plane might board late and I would get on it. At least, at the airport, I could exchange my ticket for next day, hopefully. After I waited for several minutes, the loud speaker blared that there would be no more trains to Gatwick for at least half an hour. The one that just left had derailed, and the tracks had to be cleared.

So I am a day late coming home. Fortunately, Randy could stay on an extra day, I found when I called him. Luke is fine, a happy thing to hear.

Best of all the trip was coming back to Luke. At first, he looked surprised and happy to see me, then was diffident and turned his head away, until we walked up on the ridge where he got more and more excited. And full of nuzzles when we sat on the sun porch together that evening, since it is still warm and he is sleeping there. He had been in my thoughts continuously during the three weeks I was gone, as was my family.

No cigarette butts on the road since I got back, though there were a few this summer. Randy's periodic presence may help with that. When I had talked with the sheriff's office, the sheriff himself told me that, "a woman who chooses to live alone in the middle of nowhere is asking for it," his words, not mine. They really made me mad!

1996

October 15th

The June meeting that was part of my job to organize in Montreal surprised me, and I think others, by its success. One of many results was that I was asked to coordinate a small scale, international agricultural apprenticeship program for youth that came out of that gathering and was suggested by John. I accepted and since then have been to Haifa and, on the same trip, back to Belfast for another meeting. With both Israel and Northern Ireland on my passport, I was frisked, held for questioning and bag searched at every departing airport, even with Ireland's cease fire in effect. Comically, when I flew back into Charlotte, it was my backpack the drug dog picked out from the very long line of bags being sniffed for drugs.

There were only dirty clothes in it, I knew, for the bag had not been out of my sight. So I watched with curiosity while the officer searched and found nothing, while the dog remained excited by my pack. The uniformed officer asked, "Have you had any bananas in it recently?"

I laughed at his question. "Yes, but I ate them before boarding," I told him. He laughed, too, and explained, "This dog has a particular liking for bananas and always goes for a bag that smells of them."

Diversity, everywhere, has been the very best part of traveling. That diversity is necessary to unity, or else it's uniformity, is something I think about a lot. It circles me back to this place, with its misty flora and fauna, and especially Luke, no longer so wild and very dear.

My two grand sons are now well over two and getting wild, and they are very, very dear. Sarah expects another child mid-April.

There have also been grand babies who did not make safe passage into this world, and they are part of my heart.

Luke has done well with my being gone, and I feel the bond with him even when I'm not here. With tick season over, he sleeps by my bed, though he has never shown any interest in getting up on it. And I haven't suggested it.

1997

May 10th

Another healthy grand son born in April. I went down for a
week to help with meals and Vic, a busy boy, a handsome boy almost
three, full of activity, full of questions and, even more noticeable,
quiet thoughts. Evan, his new brother, has a wonderful, wonderful
face, and I look forward to knowing him when he is not so busy
nursing. Luke went with me. He seems to enjoy going there and
occupied his usual protected corner of the stairway, with their dog
Princess friendly to him, as always. Dink the cat continues to hiss and
spit. I think it's just show, that she now trusts Luke not to attack her.
Even when he was a hunter, he never bothered Carin's cats, some of
whom still live in and out of the barn.

I do watch Luke carefully around young children and don't
leave him alone with them because there is an unknown, to me,
here. I can't imagine his hurting them, yet I have seen on our walks
together how his body can change, instantly, when he apparently gets
a scent of something and takes off. It looks as if he suddenly shifts
into a different world. Since children can fall and bloody their knees,
and I don't know if the scent of a bloody knee would switch on this
something in Luke or not, I don't chance what I don't know.

If I am close by, I am certain that I could instantly call Luke
back to his usual self and prevent anything from happening. If I'm
in another room, I ask Luke to go with me or out of doors and think
that this puzzles him. His face takes on a shadow, and I see that he
wants to be with the children. And they, him.

When I came out of Sarah's house for our return to the farm,
Luke happily came with me and trotted briskly to the Jeep. He still
springs to the high seat, though with not quite so much agility as he

used to. For at least part of long road trips, he rides in the back space where he can lie down and sleep. If Luke sleeps on the front seat, his head fills my lap which I like. But I can hardly drive, and interstates scare me enough as is. My rear view glances show that, though he will nap for a while in the back, he still watches with interest much of what goes by the windows.

November 30th

Trips, here in the U.S. and abroad, have been adventures and not too frequent. There have even been moments of romance along the way. After a conference in Honolulu last month, I spent a week in a small cottage on a neighboring Hawaiian Island and spurned the suggestion of friends to introduce me to a Honolulu man they knew of Japanese descent. I had observed that Japanese Hawaiians are a handsome and sharp people, but simply wanted to rest and swim and enjoy the view of bay from the tiny entrance porch of the rental cottage. Before I left Oahu for Maui, this man, probably not very interested himself, I thought, had sent me the message of his telephone number if I would like to call. I didn't and, midweek, he called me in Hana which is on the less populated eastern stretch of Maui.

He was interesting to talk with and we visited by phone again the next evening, though I declined his invitation to come back to Honolulu to meet. With the end of the week coming up, I acknowledged that the rental cottage had a second small bedroom. And invited him to stay in it for the weekend, if he wanted to fly over. He did.

We agreed that at the estimated time of his arrival on the small shuttle from the island's tiny airport, I would stand outside the cottage. For it stood among several unmarked cottages on a hill. To identify himself, this new friend had informed me on the phone that he was not tall, but strong from his Aikido and other martial arts training; that he could walk the streets of Honolulu at night and no one would mess with him.

I stood waiting in the bright sun of mid afternoon for him to arrive. The nearest thing to shade, besides a slim palm tree, was a tall hedge of plumeria bushes in full bloom, and I was half out of this world from their delicious fragrance. I had stood there a long time, and about decided this visitor had missed the early afternoon commuter flight, when a small van zipped into the turn off at the bottom of the hill. A youthful looking and dark headed man jumped out, saw me standing half way up the hill and beamed a smile that I could see, even without my glasses.

He turned back to the driver beside the open window and said, in a voice enthusiastic enough to carry and most likely meant to, "Look at her, she beautiful!"

That tipped me off he had felt concern, and expressed it to the driver, about what he might be getting himself into and was now feeling at least some relief. The Hawaiian man behind the wheel cheerfully leaned out the window and gave a thumbs up, that great masculine okay.

My new friend handed him some bills and grabbed a small bag from the back of the shuttle and ran up the hill. It was all an endearing exaggeration that had me laughing.

I was also happy I had put on a new, to me, sun dress from an island thrift shop. It had a sophisticated and feminine pattern on soft woven cotton that draped the figure nicely. Since I was standing mostly in sun, I also wore my woven and well traveled hat with some brim, that frame of cheek bones. This good natured admirer dropped his bag, lifted me at the waist with both hands and swung me around. Then he grabbed his bag with one hand, as we walked arm in arm up the rest of the hill, laughing together. It was a fun beginning to a fun weekend.

We swam late that afternoon in the bay just beyond the cottage, fixed supper together, talking all the while for he continued to be interesting to talk with. We spent a late evening sitting in two hard plastic chairs on the tiny porch under a full moon over water, its light and shadows still etched in my memory. Our easy conversation was mystified by the ongoing smoke of his Camel cigarettes, an aroma I remember from my father and always liked, though I never succeeded in smoking very much.

We talked late and, next morning, I slept later than usual. He woke me with a knock on the door and invitation to the breakfast he had waiting. He had shinnied up the tall palm tree in front of the cottage to pick its one coconut. Somehow, he had managed to slice off the top, and the coconut was ready for me to drink its exquisitely delicious water. He had also walked to a corner store to buy a local taro pudding that was among the best things I've ever eaten. That and a parsnip soup in a French restaurant in Galway, Ireland, some time ago!

As we had planned the evening before, this visitor and I walked after breakfast the two or three blocks to a local parade. It was a celebration of village efforts to heal domestic violence. The bright happiness overflowed both from participants riding in the parade in assorted vehicles and from villagers who lined the narrow road where the parade took place. I had a wonderful time, standing there on the hot roadside beside this new friend and watching faces of local people. I liked what I saw.

Over supper that night, I said that.

My visitor remarked he had liked standing there with me. That he could see local people were watching me and liked what they saw. A nice remark for him to make, he was good at that. In the meantime, we had spent the afternoon scrambling like goats across and down a long rock cliff to an almost out of this world natural ocean pool of deep color, among huge rocks where we swam and stretched out to sun on a boulder's warmth.

The second morning, we ate breakfast with time in mind, for both of us were catching the commuter flight back to Honolulu. From there, I would continue my scheduled return home. Just as I put a last bite of breakfast in my mouth, he was suddenly out of his seat across the table and down on his knees beside me. It is the only time in my life that someone asked me to marry him from his knees. When I had gotten over my surprise, enough to swallow that last bite and speak, I told him I wasn't saying, no. I wasn't saying anything at all because I didn't know what to say.

We agreed that we would continue to get to know each other by e-mail and, hopefully, get together mid winter. For over a year, I had used e-mail in my work. It didn't take much time for me to discover that this man, delightful as he was, and I were not right for each other. I realized it from a description of a business deal he wrote to me. It would involve breaking a law and paying a hefty fine, in order to bring on the market a product that would sell and, rightly should be available, he wrote. Since the law was unfair, he felt the breaking of it would be justified.

No, I disagreed. Even if an end is right, the means have to be consistent with it, or in the long run it just does not work, I argued.

The more we discussed the different opinion we each held, the more aware I became of how strongly I feel that means have to be consistent with the desired end. And the more I realized how deeply I believe this, the more I saw how frequently in everyday life, and without thought, I short change my belief. I remembered Carin pointing this out to me in her teenage years. At the time, I was laying down my law to her that, on our farm, she was responsible to see to it her friends obeyed drug laws. She hotly dismissed the law about marijuana, with its inconsistencies, and I didn't disagree with her but said, If that's the way you feel, work to change the law.

She pointed out to me that I broke laws all the time in small ways, by buying illegal raw goat's milk from friends (which I considered a trade) and driving just over the speed limit (not enough to get stopped). And that I wasn't doing a thing to change those laws.

I agreed she was right, and did not back down on what I insisted of her. I did stop buying goat's milk and now try to remember to drive more slowly, especially on curvy mountain roads which is where I am good at driving. The fast track traffic on interstates curbs my enthusiasm.

Since the terminal e-mails with the suitor from Honolulu, I have recognized many, and some might say unimportant, ways in which my means are not consistent with my stated (to myself) end.

But I knew with certainty, I could not marry someone who did not take seriously something that I do. Even though I scramble to live it, and he was a lot of fun.

And Luke! He couldn't move to Hawaii without a caged and surprisingly long quarantine on arrival and that wouldn't do.

1998

May 16th

Jena gave birth to a beautiful little girl last week, my first granddaughter. I spent that night with four year old Clay, a wonderful night with my arms around him who mostly slept and sometimes woke to ask if his mama, daddy and the baby were home yet from the hospital. I was there with him when they returned with lovely Kelsey and got to see Clay, who is a very appealing boy, meet his new sister and hold her for the first time. I held my granddaughter, too, though mostly kept my attention on Clay, since newborns require a lot of their mother's attention.

While I was there, he accompanied his dad who was playing banjo at the local Friday night traditional music in the nearby town. For his second birthday, Clay was given a real and small size fiddle that he has learned to bow with vigor and contagious verve. His rhythm is perfect, for he is often around old time musicians, and his small fiddle is open tuned so he doesn't have to note. He and his daddy had gone into town early and had just begun to play together on stage, when I arrived at the not too large, converted train depot building and found an aisle seat.

As I slipped into it, I saw Clay recognize me from the stage. His bright face took on even more animation and, in the middle of a beat, he set down his small fiddle and ran down the several steps to the aisle. He gathered speed as he pummeled toward me, calling out for everyone in the hall to hear, "There's my granny!"

He gave me a high spirited collision hug, ran back up on the stage, picked up his fiddle and continued to play, right on beat with his daddy who had not stopped.

Luke stayed with Carin and seemed to have his usual good time around the young adults, spirited companionship I'm sure.

July 2nd

Just at daybreak this morning or, it seemed, in that instant just before day breaks, I heard something strike my bedroom window and saw a red cardinal fly off. It could not possibly have been, could it, the cardinal that hit its feet against the window that spring Luke came, just before he arrived. That was five years ago! I have no idea how long birds can live and can see the changes in Luke. And in me. It looks to me that Luke doesn't run as fast as he used to, but then neither do I. What is more noticeable is that he seems to wait for me to start out with him on walks, instead of initiating his runs of the ridges as he used to. Once we start out together, he does take off on his own flight.

When Randy stays with Luke, he keeps him inside or on the sun porch except when the two of them walk together, long, long walks at least twice a day, Randy tells me. With Randy at work during the day, I agree that is a good idea for Luke to be inside the porch, and I can see the affection between the two of them. I also see that Luke has gotten used to staying inside more. And that he anticipates the meals I give him, though he remains lean and does not beg for food or beg for anything.

Sometimes, I do notice longing looks as I take out his chicken thigh or the yogurt container from the refrigerator. I always hold the seal of cream for him and he licks it skillfully, taking his time. He also eats beans and rice when I do and seems to like them. And some dog food, especially when Randy stays with him. What I miss is to hear Luke howl. I remember the sound, the mystery, of the one night I heard him howl.

Yet I don't know what I may be asking, I don't know what it means to a wolf or wolf/dog to howl. Was Luke singing with contentment or from loneliness or calling up something deep in his heritage? I remember reading that wolves howl to let each other, as packs or individuals, know where they are. Perhaps, Luke's howls that one night, the first spring he was here, were howls of hope. And by going out to sit on the sun porch steps to listen, maybe I was the only response.

October 7th

Everything has changed, abruptly, and I am still trying to get my bearings and know the extent of it. In early August, I was scheduled to participate in an overseas workshop, and Randy let me know in plenty of time that he would be moving onto his own farm, some distance from here. He would not be able to stay with Luke, so I made plans with a young couple. They have grazed their draft horses on these pastures and given me help with the farm and were willing to stay here the ten days I would be gone. I was concerned that their dog would come with them, yet Luke has gotten used to staying on the sun porch during Randy's stays. I asked the couple to make sure that Luke did not go outside with their dog, unless the couple, or one of them, were with them. I know that two dogs, like people, will sometimes do what one doesn't.

Somehow, Luke and their dog did go out on their own and went onto Elliot's farm. As far as I know, Luke had never gone over the line before. One of Elliot's cows had just given birth, was still bloody, and Luke attacked her. Elliot was close enough to intervene before the cow was badly hurt, the calf was unharmed. The mother recovered and, of course, I paid the vet bill. Understandably, Elliot felt for his cow that had been frightened and hurt at such a vulnerable time.

He fears that Luke, remembering the scent of blood, will come back. I am very concerned about that, too, and know Elliot will shoot Luke if he returns over the line to his farm. Elliot has told me that he will shoot Luke, if he steps one foot over the boundary, and I understand that. By custom, anyone that raises cattle in this county has that right, and I do not want it to happen. So Luke has been inside, even with me here, except when we walk together two or three times a day. My next trip away, unless Randy can stay with

Luke, I will take him to Sarah's and fly out of the large airport near her.

In the meantime, several of last summer's apprentices asked to come here during their college fall break for extended conversation on the nine points, or principles, of the apprentice orientation program. They will do some work on the farm in return for bread and board. I enjoy listening to these young adults talk about their views of the world and their concerns for it, as we linger over meals with the background hum of wood stove.

The students say they like to come because it is peaceful here, and they leave with new thoughts. Luke is a big part of their experience of this place, for the young folk notice that Luke is different from dogs they have known.

The male cardinal has continued since July to strike his feet against my window each morning that I've been here, just exactly in that moment before I see light break. He keeps hitting his feet against the glass until I sit up and speak to him through the at least partly opened window. He then lingers for an instant and flies off. I don't know what to make of it . And I don't know what to make of the change in Luke's life, in our life, and am feeling my way.

1999

January 26th

Recently, I heard again of the wolf/dog found in these mountains during the same time period as Luke. This female was not injured and not found at the same place as Luke, but in the same range of mountains that span the distance between here and Knoxville, location of the gray wolf project in the late 1980s. After learning the name of the woman who gave home to the female wolf/dog, I called and asked to come over with Luke. I didn't know, until I got there, that she had immediately thought of Luke as a potential stud for the female wolf/dog. I was wondering if her place might be a safe haven, where Luke could run free again and be in the company of another like himself.

When we arrived there and got out of the Jeep, Luke on leash, everything turned into commotion. The female wolf/dog, though not young, had a new litter of puppies and erupted with hostility at Luke's sudden presence, even with him leashed and at some distance. I was open mouthed by how alike the female and Luke looked, except that she, even from a distance, looked female, as Luke looks male. The other woman appeared equally stunned by their same markings, coloration and general size. She was also disappointed, she quickly told me, to see that Luke was neutered which saddens me too.

Both she and I felt that the two could be from the same litter, from their appearance and the little information we each had and exchanged. Yet, even if the female were to come to accept Luke's presence, I could see it would not be a right home for him. Even if the woman had wanted to take in another wolf/dog that was not a stud, it was not the place for Luke. He and I went home together, with me relieved of the decision of whether to give up Luke to what

I had thought might be a better place for him.

I have tried to imagine how things could be now, if I had not accepted jobs that have taken me away from home. It is possible, I tell myself, that Luke, sooner or later, would have ventured onto Elliot's farm anyway. More certain is that my work has been interesting and satisfying to me, that I have enjoyed the learning, the getting to know people and places, many people and places. Last month, in connection with this work, I was invited by a Lakota woman to spend several days on the Cheyenne River Reservation in South Dakota. It was an unforgettable experience and refueled my inner urgings to learn more of the grandmother I never knew, my father's mother.

I think I am beginning to understand that it is not only the lost freedom that is hard on Luke. With that, has gone his opportunity to do his work, the running of the ridges that bound this place, his marking that boundary for both of us, his chosen job.

March 22nd

Another granddaughter, another beautiful little girl, born to Mc and Lynn three days ago. She carries my long family name as her first name and is called by the whole thing, tiny as she is. And she does carry it, for she is a magical child. Mc called from the hospital, early in the first baby labor, to invite me to drive down and keep company with Lynn's mother, already there. Luke went with me since, I have learned, he takes care of himself patiently in the back of the Jeep.

After saying hello to the about to be parents in their hospital room, Lynn's mother and I were supposed to stay in the waiting room. During the wait there, evidently sensing something, she suddenly rose from her chair and said she was going to stand outside the birthing room. Though we were not supposed to, I followed her. Soon, from that hall, we heard the brief cry that sounds like a miracle and were standing there, wondering, when Mc burst from the room. His smile was wide as the world as he told us, She's a girl! And then told us her name.

Shortly afterward, I had a great privilege, as mother and grandmother, to stand on the other side of the glass nursery window where this newest member of our family was being warmed by a lamp, while her father stood tall and protective beside her, beginning to know his first child. A daughter is fortunate to have a father stand guard nearby, and a father is blessed to have a daughter to love him, as daughters will, given half a chance.

Watching them through the glass reminded me of the story of my father slipping into the hospital nursery to see me, when the nurse had gone out for a minute. She returned and chased him out, but he had managed to see me, back in those years when fathers were not invited or allowed in.

The cardinal has come back to the bedroom window now. He had disappeared during the coldest part of winter, and I like having him back.

October 5th

Luke is still his sweet self and, in important ways, still his independent self. Yet I feel concern about his inactivity, compared to the running that he used to do. On our walks together, he still walks briskly, goes off on his adventures and times his return down the ridge to start after I do. He still overtakes and passes me as he gathers downhill speed. He does this, I know, because he knows it pleases me to watch him run. And he obviously likes to run. As he flies past, I call out, "Good job, Luke!"

He stands waiting for me, looking happy too, when I reach the yard beside the sun porch and bend down to put my face against his. I know his loss of freedom is the biggest part of his lessening activity. It could very well be that lack of wild food also makes a difference. I remind myself to get up from the computer, where I work mostly from home now, to go outside more than twice a day with him. For long, long walks that I enjoy, too. The red cardinal continues to come to the window at daybreak.

2000

April 25th

    Carin was married last week, a very, very happy occasion. She and her husband, both liking the out of doors, as all my children do, chose to marry on a farm, a larger one nearby to Carin's. After a week of warm spring weather, it turned cold as could be the night before the wedding. I had left home that afternoon in light falling snow . But nothing could cool the happiness of the day, of the event, of the two families and friends present. Though tired from working many days and nights on her silk wedding dress that she asked me to make, I floated on the happy and beautiful look of her, of the smiles between her and her husband.

    All of the grandchildren took part in the wedding, my newest granddaughter just walking and growing hair. Kelsey, a year older with a head full of curls, helped her. As did the boys, all older and with important looks on their faces; with suits and ties under heavy jackets. Carin even ended up with her fleece lined denim jacket over the silk wedding dress though I had given her an Irish green wool cape. A happy, happy day.

    The cardinal continues to strike his feet against the glass of the upper part of the window each morning, until he hears my voice through the partly opened window.

2001

November 14th

    Sarah told me that she and the boys would like for Luke to live with them. It is a thoughtful offer that I think would be good for Luke, and for the boys, too. It is not the same, now, for Luke here. If Luke comes, Sarah made it clear, he stays with the boys. For their sakes, if not Luke's, no back and forth.

    I do not disagree with that, yet am using winter as an excuse to put off the decision, to delay the thought of parting with him. At the least, I want one more winter, his season, with him.

2002

February 15th

Red headed Jesse was born to Carin and Kirk on the 11th, two days after my birthday. His hair is a brighter red than his mother's, not so auburn as mine when I was born, though mine got lighter. Jesse has the blue, blue eyes of his father's family. He also has two older brothers that joined our family with their father. This newest blessing, Jesse, with his father and brothers and with his mother, Carin, and her grandfather who was my father, comes from two ancestral lines, at least two, who like to fish. So it will be interesting to see if Jesse will. He is certainly, already and always, his very own self. Like every single, individual snow flake, I have always been amazed to hear! It is snowing today. Luke and I have already walked in it, Luke danced.

Kirk had called me when he took Carin to the hospital and I left here shortly after. The drive took about the same time as the labor, and I arrived at the hospital moments after Jesse arrived. I was soon invited into the room to meet and hold my newest grandson. And to see the look of wonder, still on Carin's face, to have brought forth a miracle.

May 8th

Another wonderful gift to our family was born on the 2nd day of this month to Lynn and Mc. Young Jake already shows the quiet, handsome German heritage of his other grandparents. It always fascinates me to see past become future. And it is fun to see another pair of cousins, Jesse and Jake, the third pair close to the same age to come into our family. Again, I look forward to knowing this child, to knowing who Jake is. Our family has multiplied with blessings.

When I drove down to meet my newest grandson and take to his big sister a family doll that looks much like a newborn, Luke went with me. After our brief visit with Mc's family, I took him to Sarah's, to Vic and Evan. The boys are old enough, and I think it will be good for Luke to be around young life, to be part of a pack. It has been hard on him, here, no longer to run free. They have a wooded and roomy, fenced back yard, an adjoining park with stream and trails for families and their dog to walk. This is all I can write now, for tears blur my eyes.

May 14th

What I couldn't yet write in my last journal entry, was something that occurred as Luke and I drove out the road from this house, probably the last time that Luke will make that ride, sitting beside me in the Jeep, watching out the windows. I wanted him in front with me and close for our last few hours together. When, later, he slept for awhile, his head on my lap, I stayed in the interstate's slow lane and drove carefully.

When we had started off, we hadn't gone more than ten or fifteen feet up the road from the house, when I noticed a bright fluttering that stayed even with the passenger window, Luke's window. Though I kept the Jeep going slowly up the ridge, I soon saw that it was a red cardinal flying with exact timing alongside the Jeep, right beside Luke.

When we reached the end of the old road that enters the farm, the cardinal veered wide to the right and disappeared into woods. I stopped for a few minutes and peered out Luke's window, as did he. Trees were the only thing I could see, the cardinal did not show himself again.

It was all I could do to take my foot off the brake and put

it down again on the gas pedal. I have been back here over a week and not seen him or heard any claw taps on glass. So it must have been the same bird that has come to my bedroom window, so many daybreaks. I don't know what to make of any of this, except that I miss Luke, I miss Luke, I miss Luke.

Have kept busy finishing a request for an article about the agricultural apprenticeship program I have worked with. It will be included in a book on agricultural community development projects, to be published in London next year. The apprenticeship program has already been cited in a U.S. national publication as a successful mentoring project for young adults. Next week, I will fly out of Asheville and change planes in Charlotte for a meeting that happens to be close to London and promises to be interesting. Sheila has offered to meet me at Gatwick and take me to her home first.

Have put the gardens into cover crop for this year. The farm feels quiet in every way.

October 10th

It still seems strange here at the farm without Luke. The house feels empty, my walks lonely . This wasn't true before he came though I was alone. Then, the promise of fullness seemed everywhere, Now, I'm again finding cigarette butts on the roadbed across from the house. I visited Sarah and the boys and Luke earlier this month. He appeared to be enjoying his pack and they, him. The night before I left, Luke did not sleep in his protected corner on the carpeted steps. He stretched out beside the low single bed where I was, where Evan usually sleeps. Luke's head lay on one paw and his eyes were on me. Never had he looked so steadily into my eyes, asking me something, telling me something. I wondered what and talked quietly with him, thanked him for his years with me, for all that he has given me. And now gives to Sarah and Vic and Evan.

Before I left next morning, I stooped beside him and spoke these things to him again. Sarah and the boys had left for work and school. Luke and I were on the outside deck that circles the house, within the fenced in yard. Quickly then, for both our sakes, I walked down the few steps, went through an iron gate and started around the front of the house to the drive. Luke circled back of the house, still on the railed deck, and stood above me as I came to the Jeep door. He had expected to go with me, I could see. He must have thought his visit was completed and it was time to go home. Or maybe he was concerned about what he knew I was feeling to go without him. It still hurts to think of it.

As I stood below him, my face tilted up to him, I asked him to stay with his new family, his pack, and then made myself drive away.

2004

Another blessing arrived early this year, January 9th, another
son born to Mc and Lynn. I have been gone since then and did not
meet William until this week, William with the dancing dark eyes
of his mama. I see already that he, like Sarah's Evan, will be the
younger, bound to keep up with two just older, brother and cousin.
And like Evan he will, though Vic and Clay are quite a lot to keep up
with. And so will be Jake and Jesse. Kelsey and McIntyre, the two
girls, less than a year apart in age, quietly enjoy each other. All very
dear.

I had been gone much of these past two years and this March
again rented an island cottage, this one for a month. This one in the
Caribbean where my heart sang and danced, music that still plays
within me. In retrospect, I see clearly it was this man's generosity of
spirit that touched me so deeply. That and something about him,
happily familiar, though at first I didn't place it.

The small cottage, in a local village, was sandwiched between
a sheep farm on one side and draft horse farm on the other. Old
island houses, remnants of a sugar plantation, enclosed the rest of
the fruit filled yard. Even so, there was a distant turquoise glimpse
of tropical ocean. My first afternoon there, I looked out the window
to see what I took to be a Baja man, striding across bright grass on
the adjoining farm, with lambs jumping and frolicking along with his
firm steps. That playful scene became an imprinted memory that still
brightens my inner house. I saw it many times during the month in
the island rental house.

The following late afternoon, when again from the window
I noticed the man, I went out to the barbed wire fence and he came

over to it, lambs trailing him. I introduced myself, saying I wanted to know my neighbors, which I really did want. I wasn't just saying that.

He told me his names and spelled the last one, for it was Portuguese and tricky to pronounce and spell. He was, I later learned, a mix of European, American Indian, and likely African as part of his Portuguese heritage, the warm heritage in one person of the several people I loved so fiercely in early childhood.

From the beginning, a strong magnet drew this neighbor and me together. He felt it too, I could see in his eyes. I was also interested in his farming. He practiced, among other ideas, rotational grazing that had not yet caught on here. But which I had insisted anyone use when pasturing horses or cattle on this farm's meadows. So, I was admiring my neighbor's farm, which was obviously important to him. He worked another job week days.

A couple of afternoons after meeting him, I was down on my hands and knees on a hot day, scrubbing the kitchen floor because it stuck to my bare feet. My thick hair was tied back because otherwise it stuck to my face, and I was so damp that my sun dress stuck to much of me. From the floor I heard, rather than saw, a vehicle pull into the graveled drive. Quickly, I rinsed and dried my hands, thankful that at least I had on a brightly colored sun dress, another thrift shop purchase. This one had bold fuchsia flowers printed on well laundered and softened cotton.

I was not surprised to see my shepherd neighbor at the door. He had said, earlier in the week, that he would come by to see if I needed anything. In the meantime, I had learned that he was married, a Catholic marriage since he was seventeen, he later told me. I knew that would not change. He and his wife did not live on their property next door, but a few miles away, and she seemed to show no interest in the farm.

When I asked him in, I made a point of saying that I wanted him to see how pretty his land looked from the window wall of the cottage. I was used to being truly, and only, friends with wonderful men I have worked with.

He dutifully walked to the windows, though I could see he

only glanced at the view of his farm. I was at the other end of the rectangular room, at the cook stove taking out muffins. I had put them in to bake before I started to wash the floor. As my neighbor came into the kitchen area, I invited him to sit down for muffins and tea at the small table.

"So you cook, too," he commented.

When we finished eating, I did not invite him to more comfortable chairs as, usually, I would have. After more conversation and a reasonable time, he said he must be going. And that he would like to come back.

I replied that I hoped he would bring his wife, and again said that I wanted to know my neighbors. His eyes looked surprised.

I was surprised when the following Saturday morning, the day he usually worked long hours on his farm, he knocked at my door, alone. He stood, obviously freshly dressed and holding a narrow brimmed panama hat and a wide book. "This is a book of pictures of sugar cane farming here on this island," he held it up. "You said, you would like to hear more about my years of working the cane, when I was young. I thought you might like to see the pictures in this book," he ended his say.

I did want to see them and wanted to see him, though I seated myself in a chair rather than on the wider sofa. He set his dress hat on the sofa, pulled another chair close to mine, and opened the book. With his thick index finger, he pointed to various pictures and told me of working in sugar cane fields. "It was hard work," he said with a far look in his eyes. "Hard."

I was absorbed by the pictures and his brief story of father and older brother injured in the cane fields and unable to work, of this man taking on their responsibilities when still a teenager. I felt a tear start its slide down my face and called no attention to it.

He said nothing and reached with his wide thumb to wipe it from my cheek, a thumb with that gentleness of true strength. My father had that combination of gentleness and strength.

We sat there in our separate chairs, eyes on the pictures of the book, without saying anything at all. I felt very close to him.

When we came to the end of the book, he stood and told me he must get to the day's work on the farm. I stood to walk him to the door and, before I had any idea it was going to happen, his strong lips were on mine. I tried several times to say, "We can't do this, you're married."

Each time, his mouth covered mine and I stopped trying to talk. Then he almost whispered, "We have to find moments of happiness where we can."

For the whole long week after that, he didn't come to the fence or even wave across the fields to me. I think he was doing a Catholic penance, though we never spoke of it when he did come back. I did my own internal penance of knowing there was an extended family that would be hurt, if they knew he had visited me. And a village that would feel disappointed, for he was a man well thought of, one who visited the sick and sat with the dying. So villagers spoke of this neighbor.

Again, I thought of my belief I wasn't practicing, that means must be consistent with the end. For I have always honored marriage. Oh boy!

During my third week at the cottage, we talked over the fence and, towards the end of the last week, he came back again. I had gone out to the clothes line to get towels in, as rain was just starting. I heard the truck and walked around to the driveway side of the cottage, as he approached it. We went inside out of the rain, and I told him why I couldn't keep seeing him. I did not tell him that I was trying to decide whether or not to rent the cottage for a second month, that the cottage was available.

He stood and listened, his dark eyes somewhat down. When I became silent, standing beside him, we fell, literally, into each other's arms.

When he left, I walked to the covered back stoop with him and sat on the steps as he laced his boots. In the islands, shoes or boots are left outside. Though he had said he needed to get back to his week day job, he took a very, very long time to lace up each of the two calf high boots. I was happy that he was lingering.

We talked quietly, as rain pattered the porch roof. When, eventually, he had securely tied the second boot, he looked at me with his dark and serious eyes and said, "I will be back."

Though I had been anguishing over whether to extend the rental and delay my flight back, now I couldn't imagine leaving. I was about to consign myself to living by means not consistent with an end in which I strongly believe, that of not treading on sanctified ground, which I consider marriage to be. Now, my question became whether to stay in this cottage or find one more private. One where there would be no eyes to see him come and go, no eyes or ears to be hurt or disappointed by him or me.

Still pondering my choices next morning, I answered the ringing phone that turned out to be Sarah. Luke was having trouble with his formerly injured leg and hip and couldn't get up or down very well. She couldn't give enough time to him right now, she told me.

Having left her marriage, she had started a new job and needed to travel for it during most of April and May. It would be hard enough to make arrangements for two boys and their two animals, without a wolf/dog that needed special attention. She would have to board him at a veterinarian's for the several weeks she would be gone.

I understood her predicament, yet this was Luke! Luke, who had never, in the time I had known him, been caged. Whose spirit had been cramped enough, not being able to run free since the incident with the cow. There was no question I would go to him. Sarah and I also planned that I would stay at her house with the boys for the weeks she needed to be gone. When our call ended, I dialed the airline to confirm my flight back next day, the flight which the night before I was thinking to cancel. The decision had made itself.

As I swept and straightened the cottage to leave it, I watched for my neighbor to drive into his farm that late afternoon. From the kitchen, I saw when his truck glided along the far side of the pastures, and I went outside to the fence.

He had gotten out of the truck without seeing me and

disappeared into a chicken house and didn't come back out. I waited for what seemed a long while and then walked the perimeter of the fence on the near side of the farm, past neighboring houses, past windows, knowing my time to say goodbye was about to run out. I could imagine him getting into his truck and driving off without even seeing me.

I turned into his gravel drive, gate open, towards the distant chicken house. As I was about half way down the narrow road, he emerged and walked quickly to meet me. Close up, I first saw happiness in his face that I was there. Then other expressions, it seemed to me. Concern that other eyes were watching me come onto his place, surprise when I told him I would be leaving next day. Sadness, I thought I saw, and perhaps relief that the decision was out of his hands. Even a flash of anger, though he voiced none of these. We stood there a short while, not saying very much, then wished each other well. He took me in his strong, warm arms and held me close for a moment, despite windows and eyes. I left quickly while my legs would go.

The walk down that drive, away from moments of happiness, was among the hard things I have done in my life. Deliberately, I pushed my head tall as I could and my back straight, and kept walking. The thought of reaching Luke, while there was still time to be with him, sped me on.

The next morning, leaving for the airport, I had backed the rental car out of the drive when I remembered something left drying on the clothes line. I got out to retrieve it and saw my shepherd neighbor's truck swing into his farm. He jumped out and waved. As he hurried across fields towards me, he opened gates to the sheep enclosures as he strode. Lambs spilled out and leaped and played along with him, matching his excitement.

He knew how much I loved that sight of frolicking sheep accompanying him. It was the best goodbye he could have given me. We had moments to talk over the fence, then I had to go.

Later, as the plane climbed above the island's small airport, it went through a momentary dark air layer above ground, then rose into open sky. We half circled the island's quickly disappearing coast and, flying higher, headed towards home. Towards Luke. Towards my grandchildren, each one of them.

Still 2004

Luke and I arrived back at the farm last week, just ahead of
a roaring thunder storm and getting towards night. It was a long trip
home from Sarah's on a very hot day, though the old Jeep does have
air conditioning. Luke rode the whole way in the back, because it was
easier to half lift him into it than onto the seats. More than half lift,
and Sarah was there to help get him in. I was on my own helping
Luke out.

Luke's leg and hip were working even less well after the
five hour drive. I hadn't stopped for him on the way, had just kept
coming because I knew I couldn't get Luke back in the Jeep by
myself. Once on the ground at the farm, he did manage to walk to
the bushes and then to the small stream from the overflow of the
springs. Coming up the shallow hill to the house was hard for him
and the steps into the sun porch, almost too much. For some time
he stood, front legs on the first step and hind ones on the ground.

If I tried to lift his hips, his front legs couldn't move. If I
lifted his front legs, the hind ones buckled. Trying to raise one leg
at a time didn't work and flashes of light and thunder were rolling
closer. Finally, I remembered planks in the wood shed and helped
Luke off the steps, so that I could make a tilted bridge up the three
of them.

On the first try, Luke slid off and did not want to get back on
the slick planks. For rain had started down hard by then, the storm
was very near. Though I've never seen Luke bothered by thunder
and lightning, I wasn't going to leave him out in it, handicapped as he
seemed. Somehow, we negotiated the narrow walkway together, just
before a large flash and crack close to the house. Luke was home,
we were home. There had been days at Sarah's that I wondered if he

could make it back.

Rain was pelting against the house by the time I got Luke's bed fixed for him, and I was soaked bringing a few things from the car. Air inside the house was close, for I had been gone much of the past year. I tried both to see to Luke and find windows to open, away from the driving wind and water. The storm had brought dark, suddenly and early.

The following morning, I awoke at daybreak to help Luke out. Eastern sun shone through wild honeysuckle that had blossomed the softest orange overnight around the house, like warm light. Over recent years, what used to be grass has become a pattern of light and shadow, mostly native flora—sassafras, young hickories and maples, some oaks and birch starting, mixed with the native honeysuckle and laurel. The laurel is just starting to bloom its creamy pink next to the honeysuckle's warm radiance. Under the roof overhang of the sun porch, right next to the door, is a bird's nest, I noticed as we made our way outside our first morning back.

When Luke and I tried to walk, he could not go far at all. He would stop and stand and look at me as though surprised, himself. At Sarah's, that had been the way it was on some days, then he would have better days and, after some help in getting up, Luke would walk briskly on the path to the wooded stream on the path behind their house, trailing the sprinting boys, ahead of me. On our third day back here, he either walked or slipped down a short, but steep hill near the house.

After calling and looking for some time with increasing concern, I found him sleeping there, under the overhang of a large bush. He had little strength to help get himself back up the hill. It was all I could do to push him, carefully, up the incline and encourage him on. I had believed that, back in the mountains, Luke would be his old self again. Years ago, I held a similar hope for my father.

The last time I saw him alive, he tried to tell me he wasn't going to get over the heart failure that had been troubling him. "Oh yes, Daddy," I said, "soon it will be warm enough for you to fish again. When you get back to the river, you'll get well."

It was the last week of April then, and he had been living in Hickory over the winter to be near work. He said nothing more about it and, when I left with plans to return the following week, he stood on the front steps of the low brick rental house and blew kisses, as I drove off.

Two nights later he was gone. Then, I understood the difference I had seen in him that day and not wanted to know. The light that usually shone from his face was already going. I wish, like everything, I had listened and heard what he wanted to say, as he tried to tell me he was dying. Late in the summer before, I had responded better to an opportunity he gave me.

With my first two pretty little girls, I rode a Queen City Trailways all day, Jena throwing up over and over from the exhaust of the constantly stopping bus, to come here to see my father and my mother. For, in recent years, she had returned to live with him. Daddy met me and his granddaughters at the bus station in Statesville on that hot, August afternoon. Riding the rest of the way with him, we arrived here at the farm in time for late supper at the old pine table on the screened porch of the old cabin, not this house. I wanted my children to know the happy place of my childhood. As always, the night wall of screen wire brought close the loud, pulsing, soothing sounds of night, that rush of river over rock.

After supper, my mother washed dishes as I bathed the children and tucked them into my old bed, the iron bedstead I sleep on now. My father went out to the river to check fishing lines. When he came back to the screened porch, my mother had gone on to bed. I sat in a rocker, tired from the long and hot day, not wanting to move other than the easy motion of the rocking chair. It was dark except for a kerosene lamp, turned low, on the eating table that Lemond had made. It's light flickered slightly in the night breeze that came through the screened walls.

"Come walk with me by the river," my father said in his quiet way. "There's a full moon over it tonight."

After all these years, I remember opening my mouth to say, "Oh, Daddy, let's do it tomorrow night. I'm really tired."

Instead, I got up and went outside with him. Above the plank steps of the porch was an electric light added in recent years, a bare bulb with moths flying around its light. We walked under them and down a path to the shimmering river, then along its bank. We each had an arm around the other's back, and we talked quietly on that path beside the singing water.

He wanted to know how things were with me, for my husband, father of my children, had been ill for much of the several years we had been married. It had been extremely hard, hard for all of us. More so for him than I will ever know, I'm sure.

Towards the end of our walk, Daddy said to me that he would give his right arm, if he could go back and be with me daily during my growing up years, those years my mother took me to live in Charlotte. My head was against his shoulder as we walked, arm in arm. I remember thinking how good it felt to lean on my father.

The next day, he drove back to Hickory to work and did not return at supper time, as expected. The children and I had gathered a large bouquet of summer's end wildflowers for the long table on the porch. My mother had cooked a good meal, and we waited for Daddy to come. With no telephone at the old cabin, it was after nine that night before we learned he had been taken to a Hickory hospital with a heart attack. He got back on his feet for several months, though he never got back to the river.

Luke and I are here, though the old cabin no longer stands and Luke can no longer walk to the river. There are bluish or greenish eggs, I can just barely see, in the bird's nest over the sun porch door.

June 10th

There are baby birds in the nest. That Luke and I come in and out of the door just below the nest has been hard on the mother black capped chickadee, I can see. I try to move easily, and Luke's is always quiet. Yet our effort of getting him down or back up the steps is noise in itself. The mother bird watches from the maple tree, now grown quite tall, the one from which the rabid raccoon jumped onto Luke's back ten years ago. The same maple that Mc planted when he was a Cub Scout, and now he's grown and married, with a family. How has time gone so fast?

I see and hear the mother bird's anxiety in the way she flies and calls. And guards her babies from a distance, feeds and checks on them. I try to stay out of her way. To see the care that most animals show to their young has always touched me deeply.

June 14th

This morning as Luke and I started out the sun porch door, easily as we could, I saw two baby birds, already with markings of the black capped chickadee, on the ground. One was dead, and I thought the other was dying. He or she sat like a tiny stuffed lump though, when I bent down, I saw nearly imperceptible movement of the chest. The birds eyes were half opened. When Luke and I came back from our short walk, the baby had moved over a bit. From the outer part of the yard, I had seen the mother near it with something in her mouth.

I stopped Luke away from the porch and he, with effort, lowered himself and settled on the ground. After the mother black capped chickadee moved away from the little one on the ground and her babies in the nest above, I slipped in the sun porch door and unlocked the front door to come and go during the day. Until evening, for Luke couldn't have made it on the steeper front steps. As I went about things in the house, I worried about the baby, vulnerable on the ground just outside the sun porch. From the house windows, I saw the mother keep watch over it from the maple and fly back, at intervals, to both nest and the grounded little one.

Luke did not move from where he had laid down. Going out the front way to check on him and the baby, I could see the small bird on the ground gain strength, though he did not journey more than several inches from where I first saw him. It felt that he was a he. I didn't know if I put him back in the nest, even wearing gloves to keep my scent off of him, whether the mother would accept him. Or if he would again fall out of the nest, which had part of one side pulled away, and perhaps be killed as one of the babies had been. I didn't know what to do.

Finally, as dusk neared with the small bird still down, I put on my old soft brown cotton gardening gloves, positioned a ladder under the nest and stooped to pick up the baby chickadee. It scooted away from me, quite lively! Carefully, I folded both gloved hands around the baby and felt its fledgling strength, climbed the ladder without using my hands and placed him in the nest. There were two other baby birds in it, eyes and mouths wide open.

June 15th

The small bird stayed in the nest last night, but during this morning one of the three fell out. I'm quite sure it was the same adventurous he. Again, the baby did not fly but was more active on the ground than the day before. And, oh so lively, so brave it seemed to me. He would look up at me with obvious curiosity and no apparent fear. He ventured fifteen or twenty feet from the sun porch and appeared to enjoy watching the sunny world around him, as the day went on. I was quite taken with him though increasingly concerned that he would not or could not fly. Again, Luke stayed quietly in the background, though I could see him watching the baby with gentle interest.

Sometime in the afternoon, the little one evidently did fly, for I came out of the house and could not find him anywhere. I saw the mother go to the babies still in the nest, but she didn't hover and call from the maple any more or show agitation. Late in the afternoon, she did light on a tree near where I sat in the yard on the other side of the house. She made melodic sounds I had not heard from her before. She looked like the same bird that I had seen mothering the babies, and she was looking down right at me. She seemed to be singing something to me.

June 16th

Today, the other two little ones flew off. Earlier in the morning I was awakened in that moment just before daybreak by a dull thump and, after a minute or two, another thump, another interval and another thump. I opened my eyes, wondering if it were the mother chickadee, if something were wrong, Then, I thought, "Could the cardinal have possibly returned!" I hoped he had, yet saw nothing at the window beside my bed and closed my eyes, still sleepy.

I reopened them when the thump sounded again, saw nothing and placed the sound downstairs, under me. Getting up, I went down to the sun porch where Luke lay quietly on his bed, alert. A surprisingly large robin, with reddish orange breast puffed, sat on the step on the other side of the glass paned door and scuttled back when he or she saw me. When I opened the door to check on the two small heads in the nest above, the robin jitterbugged back and forth, sat still and watched me from a short distance, then flew off. I wondered if I had interrupted a conversation and helped Luke outside. Later in the morning, I saw that the last two baby chickadees had flown.

June 24th

That first few days back from the islands, before Sarah needed me at her house, I had opportunity for quick visits with the other three families of my children. Though Mc was off on a wind surfing trip at the coast, I saw Lynn and their children for a couple of days. Then the other two families of grandchildren and also had a day and night here at the farm in early April, when trees were still mostly bare and lacy. From the ridge tops, blue mountains rose through misty sky, birds sang spring. It was coming and so would be Luke, soon.

It had felt easy to pick back up with the older grand children. I had visited all of them last fall when Jesse and Jake were too young to remember. Since then, Jesse had turned two and Jake now is. Lynn had shown him pictures of me and helped him to say Granny, though he didn't know me. Or I, him or Jesse. Not yet, and I was meeting William for the first time and focused more of my attention on the older grand children, than the nursing baby. There is much to catch up on.

Being gone, I have missed stretches of time and moments that can never be returned to with grandchildren who grow up too fast. With Luke when we could have continued some of the things we both enjoyed, things he is now unable to do. Yet everything had changed after his attack on the cow, when he could no longer run loose without the possibility of being shot, if he set one paw over the property line. Would that risk have been preferable to him, rather than loss of freedom?

I had wanted to protect him and also felt a responsibility to my neighbor and his cows. Luke may have made another choice, if given that choice. Or, getting older, he may have been ready for a quieter life and for his two years in the pack of Sarah's family. I could see that he liked that, and that he likes these quiet times with me. Perhaps, he lives life as it comes. There are many things about Luke I do not know.

Always, I have known that he doesn't belong to me or to anyone. He is his own self, unforgettably Luke. And more and more, I realize that the creative edge of life is change, whether in an ecosystem or the everyday living of our lives. To be fully alive is ongoing change and rebalance.

Some days I walk to the river or to the top of the high ridge, though I don't like to go where Luke no longer can. Usually, I stay nearer the house, within the easier circle that he can manage. He is sweeter than ever, though it is harder and harder for him to get up off his bed or the floor or ground. For him to go upstairs is out of the question. He likes to be in the kitchen with me, though in the evening it is cooler on the sun porch. He still likes the circle of cream from a plain yogurt lid. His eyes light up when he sees me take the container out of the small refrigerator in the kitchen. He often lies with his head in my lap, both of us on the floor, either the kitchen or the sun porch floor.

July

July 3rd

Soon after I sat down here at the desk before the open window, a black capped chickadee came to the sill. It's the mother of the babies, I thought. Then looked again as the bird flew to a tree farther out, then to another tree nearer, and back here to the window over the desk. She was smaller, I looked more closely. It is the baby I had put back in the nest, I am quite sure from the jaunty way it moves. He is larger now, yet recognizable. Does he remember me? I think he does though it may be his curious nature, investigating what is moving on this side of the window screen.

June was surprisingly cool and it's still not very hot for July, or wet. Of course, the mountains always cool off at night, two wool blankets worth and more during June, less now. The river has begun to warm.

Luke on some days walks a ways on the old road bed with me, when I go to swim. I never had that part of it, from house to river, scraped and graveled along with the rest. He stops a short way down the dusty road and stands there. After I wait to see if he wants to continue and he doesn't, I move on quickly and take a fast swim.

When I come back up the narrow dirt road, Luke may still stand where I left him, head tilted downward as though about to doze in the warming sun. Or, else he is standing in the yard back at the house or somewhere between. I think that sitting or lying down is almost as hard for him as getting up. Once he gets down, we spend a lot of each day just sitting together. I miss more exercise, yet see my time with him running out.

The shade of trees growing up in the yard is pleasant and full of bird calls, and I recognize the chickadee calls. Rob's blue bird house is still on the fence post, though it has been a while since I've seen birds nesting in it. It's been a while since I saw Rob, though we keep in touch with occasional phone calls. He still makes his calls after eleven at night, and he is worth my being waked up.

July 7th

My friend since youth, John, came for supper the other night following a meeting he attended in Asheville. He and Ana, born in Portugal, have been investigating the history of Portuguese in these mountains since the mid 1560s or earlier, before an English presence here. It is a rich history that most of us know little about, other than the inclusion of Portuguese on de Soto's infamous Spanish excursion. The Portuguese were known to be good navigators.

A later expedition than de Soto's, led by Joao Pardo whom some say was Portuguese himself, established inland forts for the Spanish in these mountains about 1565 or so. An authentic and newly translated journal, John tells me, shows that the list of men who left Europe to man these forts includes at least five with the name Alonso. John brought this to my attention because he knew an early ancestor of my Cherokee grandmother was Alonso Johnson.

Alonso was the one who, most likely part Indian himself, in the mid 1700s married a Cherokee/French woman on the mountainous border of North Carolina and what became Tennessee. According to Sam's grandmother, they were the parents of Tom Johnson, my grandmother's great, great grandfather, I think it would be. Not the later Tom Johnson, her brother, who kept up a correspondence with my father after his mother died. I'm still trying to get these generations straight.

From John, I also learned that Spanish forts in these mountains were manned, apparently, by Jewish men from Portugal or adjacent Galicia, who would have taken opportunity to flee the Inquisition going on in Portugal at that time. Extant records indicate that these forts in the mountains were, early on, overtaken by native

people. If I understand John correctly, all of them were burned
in concert on the same day and at the same time by Catawbas,
Cherokees, and possibly other tribes working together. There is
good reason to think that Portuguese men who manned the forts had
already paired with Cherokee or Catawba women, which would most
likely have saved the men's lives, at least some of them. For among
the Cherokee, women had equal say in what went on. And tribal
custom shows it was understood that close kin should not pair too
closely, that bringing in new blood was important. How else would
the Portuguese name, Alonso, have come into our family?

By the late 1700s, in early census records of these mountains
and also on Cherokee rolls, I see many Old Testament names that
could be the names of Portuguese men and their descendants. There
still are what could be anglicized Portuguese names around here,
including an Alonso Johnson in the current telephone book, right
now!

It startled me when I saw it and, excited, I called the phone
of this current Alonso Johnson. The man who answered told me,
quite brusquely, that he didn't know anything about his ancestors and
didn't want to know. So I politely hung up. The surname, Johnson,
could be an anglicized "son of Joao," for Joao appears to have been a
popular Portuguese name of that time.

Luke eats less and less, yet still gets a pleased look on his
face when he sees me take the lid off a yogurt container. He licks
it slowly, lovingly, it feels to my fingers that he laps along with the
cream. I'll go do that now, for both of us.

July 13th

Yesterday, I saw a black capped chickadee fly among trees and
immediately thought it the bold baby, grown up, the bird that came
to the window last week. There is something distinctive about him.
When he circled and lit on the ground and walked toward me, I was

sure it was he. He came within two feet of my feet and looked up at me with the same bright, fearless look as that afternoon he made his way across the yard, before he flew. Carefully, I squatted down to speak to him. His recognition of me seemed obvious. Before he flew off, I saw that he looked bright and well and larger.

Last night, I talked by phone with a man who became a good friend in Hawaii. Robert, an author among many other things, is in his eighties. He has more experience, more understanding of the world than anyone I know and said to me, "The chickadee was telling you something."

That feels true, yet I don't know what the young chickadee was saying, other than he remembers me.

July 18th

Rain is pittering the tin roof and looks as if it has set in for awhile. Through the wet window glass, the yard is a stencil cutting of green. Luke is stretched out on his oval bed, here on the kitchen floor. I am writing, not at my usual desk but at the small kitchen table. It looks out to wild honeysuckle, the soft orange blossoms now spent and drowning in the rain. Though I saw a hummingbird come to one just yesterday. At distant damp woods edge, rhododendron blooms quietly and full, and I am as taken by its beauty as if I had never seen it before. As though I hadn't seen it most summers of my life.

Here and there, in somewhat open and sunny circles, green beans that I planted, are forming on their vines, good eating soon. Jena tells me that fresh beans are the best thing I cook. It's the beans themselves, picked off the vine minutes before cooking, that taste so good. I like to string and snap beans, that feel of texture in my hands.

July 22nd

I see the young chickadee at a distance, going about his life, and think I recognize his particular calls. He reminds me that those first years of living here alone were, for a while, a space of stillness. I am remembering how, gradually, I became aware of knowing when anyone entered this land a half mile away. Before I heard or saw anything rumble down this last part of roadbed. Before any sound, I would sense some change, as though deer and other wild life had suddenly stopped what they were doing to lift their heads and listen. Not that I could see them do that from the house.

After a few minutes, a car or truck would reach this descending noisy gravel road, and I would begin to hear what I had already felt. Then the car or pickup would come into view from the sun porch door or side window of this office room, where I usually write.

Luke's coming did not change such space that hung in time, though any visitor's presence did, probably because people distract me. In recent years, my own comings and goings have distracted me and brought much change. It seems to take a stillness, a space, more than any amount of time, for such sensing. And a particular place.

Is this what the chickadee has been telling me?

July 25th

The story that John told me intrigues me, that of Spanish forts in these mountains, manned by Portuguese, most likely Jewish, some at least who, with Indian help, would almost certainly have survived the burning of the forts about 1567 or so. I keep wondering how descendants of that history fit into the larger story of the Cherokees, several generations later. Cherokee who during the 1838 Removal hid out or, more accurately stated, kept place in the inaccessible Gorge. At that time the Linville Gorge was known as the wildest place east of the Rocky Mountains and, in more recent years, has been called the wildest place east of the Mississippi.

The Gorge is not far, maybe ten miles, from the archaeological site of one of the old Spanish forts, known to have been manned by Portuguese. There is more story here than I know, perhaps more than anyone living knows. A story of Cherokees like Lemond's family and ours, very likely mixed with Portuguese and Jewish ancestry, who stayed on in this area. Whose descendants did not become part of the official Eastern band of Cherokee on the Qualla Boundary. There is more story here than has been told.

I also wonder how much of his distant past Luke senses, his story. I am quite sure that he remembers things of the span of years he has been with me. There have been moments, only moments, when I have seen a sadness in his eyes, it seemed to me. What was he remembering? I still think of his howls, that one long ago night, when I heard no responding howl.

July 30th

After a pouring rain stopped at mid day, I walked down to the river while Luke napped here on the kitchen floor. Over the rushing water, I heard the song of birds that, usually, I hear around this house and had not in the dry heat of the last few days. A chorus of them called, though I couldn't see them in the dripping thickness of rhododendron and hemlocks. They sounded like black capped chickadees.

The stillness of this summer continues to bring back those years that were a special space, when Luke ran free. Though I wish for him that he could run like that now, I am thankful to have him here, asleep at my feet, the soft fur of his face against my bare toes.

August

August 3th

    In these laziest days of summer, besides picking and eating black berries as I pick, I have reread this journal started more than eleven years ago. Am putting together the scattered parts of information that could pertain to my paternal grandmother. When John was here for supper, after another Asheville meeting, he brought a point of view that could apply to her. He feels that the European's increased immunity to small pox, from generations of exposure, may have helped to keep alive an Indian/Portuguese lineage in these mountains. Some native populations were decimated by European diseases as more and more settlers arrived. Earlier Portuguese blood among the Cherokee may have made a difference.

    Of the initial information Cousin Sam gave me of the Alonso born in western North Carolina about 1730, three things caught my immediate attention because they meshed with the puzzling fragments I heard in my own family. Sam knew the story from his Indian grandmother of the half Cherokee, half French woman who married Alonso Johnson. My father made the obscure reference to his mother's family as French, that night he checked to make sure I knew I was named for her.

    Sam also described Alonso as "Deutch," as my family had spoken of my grandmother's father. I thought the word "Deutch" meant German. Now I read from several sources that to survive in these mountains after the coming of the English, people of Portuguese ancestry, often mixed with Indian ancestry, anglicized their names or classified themselves as Deutch! Sometimes they were even called, Black Dutch. Otherwise their darker hair and skin could be listed on records as mulatto and, in most locations, limit the schools their children would be allowed to attend. Segregation was still harsh when I was growing up, even when my children started school.

Lemond's 1956 death certificate called him mulatto though his mother, whose family name was Hedgepath, apparently spoke only Cherokee. Lemond's paternal grandfather, Levi, kept place in the Gorge, it is said, during the Cherokee Removal of 1838. Perhaps, because of fear of removal, people kept quiet about Indian ancestry. Have learned that the French were very present among the Cherokees during the 1600s and earlier 1700s. So my grandmother could well have had French, as well as Cherokee, ancestors and Portuguese ones, too.

A surprising thing John told me is that old Spanish records state that two American Indian women reported a settlement further into these mountains of red haired and blue eyed people, said to have been there earlier than known European presence.

Incidentally, I've heard Cherokees say that children with a Cherokee parent and a Caucasian one are often born with red hair! My father's hair was auburn. His eyes were brownish or hazel, not blue. My eyes usually look greenish and my hair was auburn when I was born, then became a reddish light brown, when not sun bleached as usually it was. How much is from our Irish line and how much otherwise? Some people comment with surprise that I have olive skin. What does that mean and why does skin color mean anything?

I wish like everything, I could talk with Sam about all of this and get his take, that I had asked him more before he died. I am on my own figuring out the rest of my unknown grandmother's story, its subtle shadow.

Will go turn my attention now to Luke.

August 9th

When I help Luke up, he seems to like our slow walk to the bushes across the roadbed from the house, then to the small stream that comes from the springs. He stands there in the fresh, moist air that comes off that shallow run of water, a dampness I like, too.

Jaunty, orange Turk's cap lilies bloom lush in such damp, sunny spots at woods edge. And each set of the three large green leaves of white trillium, long finished blooming, now carries one grape size, bright red seed pod. Joe Pye weed shows quiet purple along the river bank and tugs my heart with memories.

August 16th

With Kathy no longer in this area, I know of no vet willing to come out to see Luke. Not only would it be very hard for me to get Luke into the Jeep, it would be hard on him. Even if I could get help, I feel it would upset him to be taken in and out of a vehicle and then into a strange vet's office. I want what are almost certainly his last months, or weeks, to be peaceful. He does not appear to be in pain, except when getting up or down.

In a phone conversation last night, John told me something else that he had read. Earlier Indians in northwest Georgia, probably in this whole mountainous area, considered the black capped chickadee to be a messenger bird! I had told John about my experience with the small chickadee.

He also emphasized that Lemond is a Portuguese name, a Portuguese surname, though local pronunciation is like the fruit, lemon. Yet, Lemond's grandfather is said to have been among Cherokees who maintained place in the Gorge during the 1838 Removal of southeastern Indians to what is now Indian Territory in Oklahoma. His given name, Levi, could be an indication of Jewish and Portuguese heritage from Galacia, mixed with the Cherokee known in Lemond's family.

And ours? One of the earlier Tom Johnson's sons was Abraham, another, Hyram, both Biblical and possibly Portuguese Jewish names. Ella, my grandmother's middle name by which she was called, is a not uncommon Cherokee name and is similar to the Portuguese word, "ela" which means woman, if I'm remembering correctly, maybe earth. Maybe both.

The only thing I've found about my grandmother's mother, other than Sam's insistence that she would have been Indian, perhaps confirmed by the silence about her, is a circumstantial tie between her and Lemond's paternal grandfather or grandmother. It appears, from census records, that Levi and his wife, Caroline, moved to Kansas to be near my grandmother's widowed mother and her children. If so, they carried out the responsibility that my father's Uncle Tom took for him, the traditional responsibility of a man for a sister or her child, the responsibility of a Cherokee who knows the traditional matrilineal clan system. It was matrilineal, not matriarchal, a difference that was a matter of balance.

This could explain why Levi and his wife, in the years following the Civil War, moved to war ravished Kansas near where my grandmother and her mother stayed after the father was killed. Lemond's great granddaughter, too, was aware of her ancestor's move to Kansas and perplexed by it. After Levi's death, his wife, Caroline Paine, is listed on an official western Cherokee roll. My grandmother's mother was most likely a sister or niece of either Lemond's grandfather or grandmother.

Many things about my grandmother's history fit with Cherokee history. Her father fought for the Union in the Civil War, as did many or most Cherokees in the western Cherokee Nation. His wife and children left for the Neutral Territory in Kansas after the war started, at the same time and place to which thousands of Indian war refugees fled from Indian Territory.

The oldest brother of my grandmother, Tom Johnson, returned from Kansas to western Indian Territory and later, from there, wrote his letters to my father back east. In doing so, he carried out a Cherokee man's responsibility to oversee his sister's child. If all of these things are coincidence, it is a lot of coincidence.

Most telling is that my grandparents, some time after their 1885 marriage in Kansas, came back to northwestern Georgia. Cherokees had been torn from there by federal soldiers nearly fifty years before, held at length in cruel and crude, open and unsanitary stockades, marched at gunpoint without adequate food or clothing on the "trail where people cried," so Cherokees call it, though at least 4000 died. Cherokees say that it was settler families who cried, as they watched the Cherokee go past.

It comforts me, to think that European settlers cried for native people. I've heard, also, that some local settlers helped to feed Cherokee women and children staying out of sight on remote mountains during and after the Removal. It also interests me that the man my grandmother chose to marry had a grandmother who, though partly Irish, grew up among the Potowami and Miami Indians of Indiana. Was she part Indian herself?

My grandfather most likely knew his grandmother's story, when he left Indiana for Kansas and married Ella Johnson. In another coincidence, the Federal government had by that time moved the Potowamis from Indiana to Kansas! He would most likely have known that. I wonder what family story lies quietly there.

There is another tie, a confusing one, of my grandparent's two families to each other and to the family of Lemond. These three surnames were combined in two different ways in the first and last names of Sam's kin, also my kin, in Missouri where my grandmother was born in that southwestern corner next to the Cherokee part of Indian Territory.

One relative had the last name of Lemond's family as a first name with Johnson, my grandmother's maiden name, as his surname. The other had Johnson as his given name and the surname of my Irish grandfather! This is documented information that suggests other marriages or ties among these three families before the marriage of my grandparents. Other generations of friendship and kinship before that of Lemond and my father. The three families of my two grandparents and Lemond's evidently had known each other for some time, for several generations at least.

No wonder Lemond meant so much to me, besides the fact of who he himself was, and that he was my father's friend and fishing companion, both of them so important to my young life.

These family histories must have influenced my grandparents, too. For, several years after they married and before the 1896 birth of my father, they reversed that trail of tears. Together, they came back to a particular place, to north Georgia that had been a Cherokee place. And, later, my Daddy and Lemond ended up with cabins across the same narrow river, this river right here in the North Carolina mountains. This rushing river that I will always remember as a lightning lit ribbon in the night, where Joe Pye now bloom full and purple along it.

This river and wild gorge, where local people say Cherokees held place during the Removal of 1838, are located no more than ten or fifteen miles west of where archeological evidence now promises to reveal that, in the latter 1500s, at least one of Joao Pardo's Spanish forts was over taken and burned by native people. The mixed heritage that could have resulted, from American Indians and Portuguese, brings back to me the shepherd neighbor on the island, that something in him so familiar to me. That something that attracted me to him. And him to me.

August 24th

Two nights ago Luke had a heart attack, I think it was. From my bed over the kitchen, I heard loud knocking noises and immediately went down to check on him. Luke was lying on his side, his body jerking with what looked like seizures that rhythmically jerked his head back against the wall. I pulled him away from the wall and lay down between him and the wall, away from his thrashing and still formidable legs, with my right arm around him. My hand was over his heart, as I held him close to my mine.

After another ten or more minutes, the jerking stopped, Luke breathed more easily and relaxed against me. We both slept there on the old linoleum floor, one of my arms still around him, the other under my head for a pillow. The following morning, he seemed himself, except weaker and unable to help get up off the floor.

By the weekend, I was nearly exhausted from lifting him, spot bathing him when needed, checking on him during the night, wondering what to do for him. I tried again to find a vet who would come to him and couldn't. Carin and part of her family arrived on Sunday to help for the day. She took care of Luke with young Jesse's help, and Kirk's oldest son did a masterful job of digging a grave. For we could all see that it is only a matter of time. The grave is deep and between two boulders that will be beautiful markers, a hard grave to dig. A hard grave for me to see waiting, help that I am very thankful for.

Today, there is beginning a feel of fall in the air.

August 27th

Luke sleeps during the day a lot, and I have continued to put together family information like a many pieced puzzle. Suddenly, I think I understand that it wasn't just the missing of my father and Lemond after I was taken to Charlotte to live that made me feel unsure of which way was up and which, down. I simply did not realize then, that I was between two cultures or more, each with very different ways of seeing the world. It was the not knowing, the not being able to name what was confusing, that was the shadow. Like Luke, like countless people, I danced with very different ways of being in the world, of seeing it.

I remember the opinion about wolf hybrid puppies, that it is particular genes inherited, rather than blood quantum, that determines whether each puppy acts or looks more like a wolf or a dog. I don't know about my genes. It may have been simply that I knew Daddy and Lemond and liked what I knew. Perhaps, I learned from them because they made sense to me, as Luke makes sense to me. Daddy and Lemond were each, in different ways, caught between different worlds, too.

As was Lemond's son Joe, especially Joe, who was a soldier during World War II. He, perhaps, never completely recovered from the physical injury, a chemical injury, still not well understood or compensated for or fully recognized as the injury it is.

Luke died in my arms yesterday morning, a little over eleven years since he came to me. By the vet's estimate of Luke's age at that time, he lived thirteen or fourteen years. It still takes my breath away that he is gone. On the kitchen floor, I had been holding him in my arms for over an hour before he died. He looked content as I held him close and said, "Go free, Luke. Go free, my friend."

I had said that to him last week, in the wee hours of morning when I held him against me, as he went into spasm after rigid spasm I didn't think he would survive. We had one more week together before he did go.

Luke first came in a dream, that early morning over a decade ago, the day the blizzard of '93 started. He came again this morning, for very early I awoke from a different dream of him. He was lying on spring green grass and lifted his head with that usual look of interest, shown in his up slanted eyes and by the angle he held his head. In the brief dream, so real, he got up easily, with his old strength and grace, no sign of the increasing disability he has shown in recent months. Then Luke ran, just like he used to. He ran like the wind into a distance of dream.

Fresh morning air came through the opened bedroom windows, along with colors of sunrise. I lay there in bed watching and remembered the cardinal that used to strike his feet against the glass. I thought about Luke, no longer downstairs in the sun porch, waiting for me to let him outside. I was comforted by the dream that awakened me, as Luke ran free. Comforted that something, somewhere, let me know that, somehow, Luke is all right, he is free. It is what I kept saying to him the last hour of his life in my arms, just yesterday and yet a world away, "Go free, Luke. Go free."

The sweet wild spirit of him will, for me, always run ridges in the wind.

Epilogue

Here in the mountains, I often walk up the incline behind the house to Luke's grave, on which I planted an evergreen virburnum, now a small and graceful tree. Underneath it are Oriental Eye iris, because they are pretty and the name reminds me of Luke's up slanted eyes. I sit on one of the large rocks on either side of the grave and think, "Here lies Luke."

Then I know, Luke lies here in my heart, as my hand goes to it. We are changed by what we love. It becomes part of us and, in this way, lives on.

Afterword

Some may ask, is the story true?

Luke was a real wolf/dog and everything in the story actually happened. Time was sometimes telescoped, actual places combined, some names were changed. Some things were left out to give focus. The story is true.

About the Author

Nancy E. McIntyre, who gave home to Luke, the wolf dog, has lived in the mountains of North Carolina on and off all her life, always returning to them. She now lives in a small cabin with no electricity or running water, adjacent to the Black Mountain range.

She grew up on the Linville River and has a particular interest in mountain rivers, native plants, and native animals. The mother of grown children, she was an early advocate of local, sustainable agriculture and has participated in Baha'i international meetings on the importance of agriculture and the work of the farmer.

CPSIA information can be obtained
at www.ICGtesting.com
Printed in the USA
BVHW031635090620
581030BV00003B/109